The Radiance of a Thousand Suns:
THE HIROSHIMA PROJECT

A Drama With Music

by

ANNE V. MCGRAVIE, DWIGHT OKITA,

NICHOLAS A. PATRICCA and DAVID ZAK

Dramatic Publishing

Woodstock, Illinois • London, England • Melbourne, Australia

"This is Your Moment"
Music by
CHUCK LARKIN
Lyrics by
DWIGHT OKITA

Cover design by Susan Carle

ISBN 0-87129-792-2

FOREWORD

The anniversary year 1995 started out badly. Veterans of World War II were still furious at President Clinton for asking the postal service to withdraw a stamp commemorating Hiroshima. The veterans had looked forward to seeing that stamp issued later in the year to mark the fiftieth anniversary of the end of World War II. The atomic bomb, they felt, had saved their lives by quickly ending the war. They wanted to celebrate their relief at being spared, and a postage stamp showing a mushroom cloud over Hiroshima seemed most appropriate. Withdrawal of the stamp renewed animosities that had simmered against the Japanese for fifty years.

The American Legion and its three million members vented their anger by attacking the Smithsonian Institution, where a display on the Enola Gay, the B-29 bomber that had dropped the atomic bomb on Hiroshima, was about to open. The aircraft's mission had arguably left a greater imprint on world history than any other 20th-century event. The Smithsonian's National Air and Space Museum wanted to recall the war that had led to the bombings of Hiroshima and Nagasaki and describe their dangerous legacy—huge arsenals of nuclear warheads threatening unimaginable destruction. This was not a theme the veterans would tolerate. Calling on supporters in Congress, the Legion exerted intense pressure on the Smithsonian and cowed the Institution into canceling the exhibition. Though the exhibit had never been allowed to open and nobody had ever seen it, it ignited a year-long media fire storm fueled by hundreds of articles in the national press, countless radio talk shows, and worldwide television coverage.

This was not the only dispute raging across the country that year. The mood in Washington was turning ugly; the Congress and President were leveling increasingly shrill accusations at each other and reasoned debate was giving way to violent dispute and frantic lobbying. By the fall of 1995, the government of the United States had been shut down as the Congress sought to force its views on the President by withholding the budget to maintain government services. Federal workers all over the country were sent home and for weeks the nation faced a stalemate.

This is the atmosphere in which *The Radiance of a Thousand Suns: THE HIROSHIMA PROJECT* premiered at Chicago's Bailiwick Repertory on July 16, 1995 (as: *THE HIROSHIMA PROJECT*). The date had been chosen to coincide with the fiftieth anniversary of man's first nuclear blast—the *Trinity* test at Alamogordo, New Mexico. The play's run was timed to remind audiences of the devastation, fifty years earlier, of Hiroshima and Nagasaki on August 6 and 9, 1945. Despite the public outcry against the Smithsonian's intended exhibition and partly to protest its suppression, the Bailiwick was staging a work which openly dealt with Hiroshima. Nicholas Patricca's play, written with Anne McGravie, Dwight Okita, and David Zak, deliberately tackled this persistent American taboo.

The United States would like to forget the atomic bombings. They do not easily fit our national self-image—a portrait of a nation that is generous to its friends, charitable to its enemies, and unwilling to use force except in defense of its democratic ideals. Hiroshima refuses to fit that kindly picture, and this confuses, annoys and even enrages us. Though the atomic bombings have transformed world history for centuries to come, we are unable to find common ground for openly discussing their history or legacy. Failing to do that, we are unprepared to unite, to intelligently debate and define a rational course to deal with an increasingly complex future.

The weapons of mass destruction we now possess could unleash catastrophes a million times more widespread than

4

those that obliterated Hiroshima and Nagasaki. We now have fifty thousand warheads, many a hundred times more powerful than those dropped to end World War II. Restraint from using them will require a wisdom that still eludes us. Where will we find the moral standards to deal with these arsenals of mass destruction we have wrought?

Americans tend to take our good fortune for granted. Our democratic form of government has persisted for over two centuries and we assume it will last forever. This hubris threatens national tragedy. More than a year after the breakdown of government in 1995-6, the country still has not fully absorbed the lesson that national problems do not go away without open discussion and consensus. Debate and a respect for others' views are basic to a democratic way of life.

The social significance of theatrical plays, exhibitions, and other works of art, lies in their ability, through the use of staging, objects, images and sound, to provide insights into divisive issues that defy conventional debate. Art, in this way, can help democracy flourish by sustaining debate and a search for consensus. When artistic ventures or attempts at public education are suppressed, dismissed as "politically correct," or excised from public view, we endanger the process.

The Radiance of a Thousand Suns unflinchingly asks crucial questions. If it provides no pat answers nor a reassuring ending, that is as it should be. The visitor leaves the theater aware that we do not yet know how the Hiroshima story will end, nor whether a playwright will survive to record it.

Martin Harwit

Martin Harwit is the former director of the National Air and Space Museum, Smithsonian Institution, Washington, D.C.

THANK YOU

The making of this play involved the support, spiritual and material, of many people. In this brief space, the authors would like to mention just a few to honor those named and unnamed: Sr. Theresia Yamada, Frank Triggiano, David Slavsky, Patsy Felch, Kathleen McCourt, Cecilie Keenan, David and Karen Cortright, Chris and Sue Sergel, and Martin and Marianne Harwit.

The Radiance of a Thousand Suns: THE HIROSHIMA PROJECT was supported in part by special assistance grants from the Fourth Freedom Forum, Loyola University Chicago, International PEN San Miguel Mexico Chapter, and the Chicago Artists International Program.

AWARDS

After Dark, "Best Ensemble," 1994-95 Chicago Theatre Season.

Joseph Jefferson Committee, Citation for "Outstanding New Work," 1995-96 Chicago Theatre Season.

The Radiance Of A Thousand Suns: THE HIROSHIMA PRO-JECT was first presented at the Bailiwick Repertory in Chicago. The production was directed by David Zak and included the following:

CAST / ENSEMBLE

Brooks Darrah . . . . Richards, Wigner, Oppenheimer, Feynman, Goudsmit, Groves, Actor 5

Alyson Horn . . . . Maggie, Keiko, Actor 3

Timothy Jon . . . . Daniels, Slotin, Harwit, McCloy, Agent, Churchill, Actor 4

Gabriel Lingat . Reverend Minaga, Intelligence Officer, Actor 7

Carol Luat . . . . Yumi, Michiko, Actor 6

Joel Sanchez . . . . Physicist

Dan Smith . . Tyler, Szilard, Yoshiro, Fr. John, Teller, Actor 1

Genevieve VenJohnson. . . . . . Einstein, Roosevelt, Truman, Sr. Theresia, Woman in Commercial, Actor 2

PRODUCTION STAFF

Dramaturg . . . . Nick Patricca

Stage Manager . . . . Margot E. Eccles

Lighting Design . . . . Robert Dalleska

Sound Design and Musical Arrangement. . . . . . Bob Garrett

Composer ("This is Your Moment") . . . . Chuck Larkin

Lyricist ("This is Your Moment") . . . . Dwight Okita

Costume Design . . . . Michael Alan Stein

Production Assistant and Curator. . . . . Ellen Ushioka

Assistants to the Director . . . . Joel Duran, John Rogers

A NOTE FROM THE DIRECTOR

The Bailiwick production of *The Radiance of a Thousand Suns: THE HIROSHIMA PROJECT* was staged elegantly and simply. Eight black chairs were positioned in front of an 8' x 20' black wall. At the start of the performance, the playing areas for the different parts of the piece were discrete: the physicist, DC; the young women, L and R; and the musical sequence, "elevated" by having the actors standing on their chairs to create a bizarre, upper-level "TV studio." As the action of the play developed, actors from one area integrated into the next, leading to the final sequences in which the actors worked in counterpoint to the previous sections.

Our costumes were also simple: black and grey casual wear, augmented by an occasional pair of glasses or a simple prop, such as a kite. Robert Dalleska's lighting design served our work excellently with wonderfully "ballet-like" color washes and side light. As this was a feast for the ear, we relied on sound design to move us from Japan to Scotland, carefully underscoring the change in date and time. Finally, the sound effect of the bomb was tremendous, earth-shattering, and heartbreaking in its own right—as you heard the air split, explode, and the fire storm consume the stage.

Our production relied on a tremendously committed group of actors to communicate the horror and the hope of this great event of world history. It is our hope that your production will also find its own proper human path to the heart of the meaning of this overwhelming reality.

8

The Radiance Of A Thousand Suns: THE HIROSHIMA PROJECT

A Play with Music
For 4 Women and 4 Men*

CHARACTERS

ACTOR 1 .. Tyler, Szilard, Yoshiro, Fr. John, Teller, ensemble

ACTOR 2 ..... Einstein, Roosevelt, Truman, Sr. Theresia, Woman In Commercial, ensemble

ACTOR 3 .... Maggie, Keiko, ensemble

ACTOR 4 ...... Daniels, Slotin, Harwit, McCloy, Agent, Churchill, ensemble

ACTOR 5 .... Richards, Wigner, Oppenheimer, Feynman, Goudsmit, Groves, ensemble

ACTOR 6 .... Yumi, Michiko, ensemble

ACTOR 7 .. Reverend Minaga, Intelligence Officer, ensemble

PHYSICIST............................. ensemble

* Minimum number for the ensemble which may be enlarged for the specific production. Musicians may also be added.

9

IMPORTANT BILLING AND CREDIT REQUIREMENTS

ACT ONE

"I Am Become Death, Destroyer of Worlds"

PHYSICIST. At the fifth hour, the 29th minute, the 45th second, on 16 July 1945, a searing light scorched the New Mexico desert...a new light, never before seen, rose on the Sangre de Cristo Mountains. Though we had prepared two years for it, when the moment came, we forgot to wear our goggles. The light blinded us. We turned our heads away: first from the light, then from the hot air blast. My glasses were blown off my face. The explosion was many times stronger than we expected. It exceeded our wildest guesses. We jumped up and down like little kids. I ran around shouting war whoops as if we were playing cowboys and Indians. Then I saw the cloud, the rising mushroom cloud. "My God, My God, My God."

OPPENHEIMER. "I am become Death, Destroyer of Worlds."

PHYSICIST. Dr. Robert Oppenheimer, our scientific director, looking at the cloud, remembered this line from the Hindu scripture, the Bhagavad Gita: "I am become Death, Destroyer of Worlds." For a moment I thought we had set fire to the atmosphere and I was watching the destruction of the earth. This was merely a remote, a very remote, mathematical possibility, but, we had no idea... you must understand the nature of science...there's a profound difference between a theory and an experiment, between an experiment and a real-life situation...this was the first nuclear explosion in the history of the world. Code name: Trinity. Place: Alamogordo, New Mexico, July 16, 1945. This was the first of three atomic bombs. We had two bombs left: "Little Boy" and "Fat Man." One down, two to go. In his last public speech, Einstein expressed his regret at ever having written the equation: $E = mc2$.

EINSTEIN. Concern for man himself and his fate must always form the chief interest of all technical endeavors—in order that the creations of our mind shall be a blessing and not a curse to mankind. Never forget this in the midst of your diagrams and equations.

PHYSICIST. Even he hadn't understood. Even Einstein hadn't understood what it really means to say that matter and energy are interchangeable, that matter can be transformed into energy, that one handful of sand can produce enough electric power to light up the entire world for thirty days.

Imagine: each grain of sand a tiny sun, a powerhouse of energy.

He said. In his last public speech, Einstein said he "should've been a plumber." He said...

EINSTEIN. "I would've been a damn good plumber too."

* * * *

OPENING SCENE OF "THIS IS YOUR MOMENT"

REVEREND. The topic of my sermon today is—HISTORY. Which is, of course, the science of how we remember things. It is an inexact science, to say the least.

For example, Mr. Komachi and I, here, first met 14 years ago. This much we agree on. But he insists that we first met at a church picnic; while I distinctly recall we met fishing by the sea. There is no account of our meeting that will satisfy either of us.

August 6, 1955—just a few months away—will mark the 10th anniversary of the dropping of the atomic bomb on Hiroshima. This event too will be remembered in a variety of ways. Since it's unlikely there will ever be a consensus on what happened in that historical moment and why—the least we can do is make as good a picture as possible so that one day the truth might emerge.

I have been asked by the host of an American television program to come to Hollywood to speak about my Hiroshima Maidens Project. We are still in negotiations. The name of his show is ... "THIS IS YOUR MOMENT." I have never heard of it before, but I think the name has a very ZEN-like quality: "THIS IS YOUR MOMENT." Don't you think so? At any rate, if I decide to appear on his show—I will be in Hollywood at the end of the month.

I hear Hollywood is a strange and magical place. I like strange places. They remind me ... of Hiroshima.

Now, will you please join me in singing our favorite hymn.

(REVEREND starts singing, ENSEMBLE joins in. [The traditional spiritual "Amazing Grace" was used in the Bailiwick production])

* * * *

LETTER A

YUMI. Edinburgh, Scotland, The United Kingdom, beyond The Continent of Europe.

YUMI & MAGGIE. The World, The Universe. The twenty-third of April 1939.

MAGGIE. Dear Yumi, If only you could see me. I'm wearing kimono. Yes, kimono! With the most beautiful white chrysanthemum painted on it. I think I'll keep you guessing about why I'm wearing it— No, I won't. I'm Princess Chrysanthemum in ... *Princess Chrysanthemum*! An operetta which Daddy calls "ersatz Japanese." But I get to sing and dance—well sway, then.

(The GIRLS come together for blood sister ritual—they put thumbs together and pivot hands up and down. This is the only time they touch.)

Oh, it's all so lovely ... The other girls get to wear them too, of course, and they're saying stupid things like, "Oh, how lovely! I get to wear a kimono!" I said, "You're all being unbelievably stupid, you know. In Japan, they say, kimono. Not *a* (ah) kimono, not *the* kimono. Kimono." Oh, Yumi, I'm so lonely because I don't know anyone. Daddy says a war's coming. He left yesterday to join—what else?—the Royal Engineers. And Mummy's forever at meetings of the Red Cross and air-raid wardens. Stupid. But Daddy says the war won't last. Hitler's just a big boast. Then we can return to Japan. Won't that be too, too unbelievable! Pat Mrs. Hachiya's cats for me. Do they still wear the little bells we bought them? Love, Maggie.

P.S. Is Yoshiro still pretending to ignore you when he rides past on his bike every morning?

Sayonara, Your lonely and homesick-for-Hiroshima Maggie.

* * * *

PHYSICIST. An Atom is a unit of matter, the smallest unit of any element. It consists of a central, positively charged nucleus surrounded by a system of electrons, equal in number to the number of nuclear protons. The entire structure has an approximate diameter of one /one hundred millionth of a centimeter, and characteristically remains undivided in chemical and physical reactions. For years, the English physicist Ernest Rutherford had been firing alpha particles at atoms, trying to pierce the armor protecting the nucleus. Then, one day, in 1932, while conducting similar experiments at Cambridge, James Chadwick discovered the neutron, an entirely neutral particle. The neutron, because it is neither positively nor negatively charged, could easily enter the atom with almost no resistance at all.

(Lines can be divided among the ENSEMBLE. [This was the Bailiwick division])

ACTOR 1. Leo Szilard, a physicist and a Jewish refugee from Hungary, was among the first to understand. "It occurred to me," he said, "that a chain reaction might be set up if an element could be found that would emit two neutrons when it swallowed one."

PHYSICIST. Upon reading about the experiment conducted in Berlin by Otto Hahn and Fritz Strassmann,

ACTOR 2. Madame Irene Joliot-Curie in Paris

ACTOR 3. and Fräulein Lise Meitner in Stockholm

ACTORS 2 & 3. simultaneously hit upon the idea that

ACTOR 3. large,

ACTOR 2. unstable,

ACTOR 3. heavy

ACTORS 2 & 3. atoms found in radioactive elements,

ACTOR 2. such as uranium,

ACTORS 2 & 3. would be the perfect stuff for nuclear

ACTOR 3. fission which is what Dr. Meitner named it in analogy to the multiplication of bacteria.

PHYSICIST. As far as we know, the atom was split first in Rome in 1934. But no one understood what they had done.

ACTOR 4. Emilio Segrè, at the funeral of his teacher Enrico Fermi, said: "God, for His own inscrutable reasons, made everyone blind at that time to the phenomenon of nuclear fission."

PHYSICIST. Lucky for us. Hitler and Mussolini were suspicious of theoretical physics, which they considered a Jewish science. The physicists of Italy and of central

Europe fled to the United States. First to Columbia University, then to the University of Chicago.

ACTOR 1. It isn't just a problem of splitting the atom, getting two for one;

ACTOR 4. you also have to catch on average more than one of the escaping neutrons and get them to enter another atom.

ACTOR 2. If you don't catch enough of the escaping neutrons,

ACTOR 3. you don't get a self-sustaining, exponential build,

PHYSICIST. you don't get a chain reaction, you get a fizzle.

ACTOR 1. Again Leo Szilard was among the first to understand what was really going on. He asked atomic physicists throughout the world to keep secret their knowledge of the possibility of nuclear chain reaction. *(Pause.)*

PHYSICIST. What Szilard asked was so contrary to what scientists had spent their lives working for: freedom of information, the very life blood of science. The secret could not be kept. The Kaiser Wilhelm Institute in Berlin started to stockpile uranium.

* * * *

LETTER B

YUMI. Hiroshima on the Sea of Japan, Empire of Japan, The World, The Universe. The twenty-ninth of May 1939.

Dear Maggie, I hope you do not laugh at my English letter or say it is stupid. If you do, I ask you write next letter in Japanese. Be warned, Maggie. I hope you do not have war, because war is very, very stupid, as you will say. My father say Japan war with Manchuria too long and wasteful. But he think and hope it must end soon. Surprise! You are princess of chrysanthemums! I remember how big your eyes grow when you first see lovely big Japanese chrysanthemum. Surprise! I also wear kimono as I write letter. I just return with mother from tea ceremony at house of Mr. Ogura. I know it would please you.

(Blood sister ritual.)

I wear kimono of Grandmother. It smell very old but has two beautiful cranes on back. I wish to send Grandmother's cranes to Scotland to bring you good health and happiness and keep you safe from war. Sayonara, your true friend, Yumi.

I forget to say Yoshiro smile at me sometimes. But smile at others too. Sometimes I truly hate him and sometimes I think my heart to break.

* * * *

PHYSICIST. Once again, this amazing man, Leo Szilard, took the world into his hands. Convinced that the Nazis had understood the implications of chain reaction for military purposes, he jumped into his old wreck of a car and set off for Princeton.

(Two chairs are moved together to become the automobile.)

SZILARD. Wigner, where's Einstein?

WIGNER. In Long Island somewhere. He spends the summer months on the beach.

SZILARD. Take me there.

WIGNER. I've never been there.

SZILARD. So what? Let's go.

WIGNER. I don't know where he stays. Look at the map. Long Island's a big island.

SZILARD *(on phone)*. Operator, Long Island, New York please, and fast.

WIGNER. The house is not in his name. It belongs to a friend of his.

SZILARD *(on phone)*. Long Island? Wait a minute. *(To WIGNER.)* So, what's the friend's name?

WIGNER. Richardson, Robertson, Roberts, Richards, something like that.

SZILARD. Operator, how many Richardsons you got? What city? *(To WIGNER.)* What city?

WIGNER. Starts with a "P."

SZILARD *(on phone)*. Starts with a "P." You got that many?! Pick one. OK, how many Richardsons you got there? How many? *(To WIGNER.)* She's got 31 Richardson's in this town. *(To OPERATOR.)* Try another town. Any town. Try Robertson. That many? Wigner, you got to do better than this.

WIGNER. Best I can do.

SZILARD *(hangs up phone)*. Let's go. We'll find him.

* * * *

LETTER C

MAGGIE. The twenty-third of October 1939.

Dear Yumi, The war did find us. Exactly one week ago. What excitement! A dogfight between two fighter planes broke out over Edinburgh! We actually watched as the bullets fell all around us! The German plane was shot down into the sea. The pilot was rescued, and one of the girls swears she saw him picked out of the water and one of his eyes was hanging out—but she likes to exaggerate. After that, some of the girls were sent away from Edinburgh by their parents. —Did I tell you? Little children have been evacuated from all the cities to keep them safe if there's any bombing.— Anyway, most of the girls have returned because nothing has happened here since.

For a while we had classes in the blacked-out first-floor library. You can't imagine how awful it is to sit with all the windows painted black at the edges and hung with horrible thick black stuff to keep the windows from blowing out. We have air-raid drill twice a week. We go to the shelter under the school and sit looking very stupid in our gas masks. However...there's a big jar of sweets kept in the shelter, and we each get one to eat.

Because sweets and chocolates have almost disappeared from the shops, we appreciate the sweet. But only one sweet?

Your grandmother's kimono sounds lovely. Will you let me wear it—just once—when I come back to Japan?

Mummy, who relied on Daddy for everything, is now running the war on the homefront. Don't laugh. Her tin hat with a big W—for warden—hangs in the hall—above the pail of sand, kept at the ready to put out any incendiary bombs that fall on the roof. *(Laughing.)* Really stupid... Don't forget me, Yumi. Maggie.

P.S. I *know* Yoshiro likes you the best. He's just shy.

P.P.S. I'm still waiting, searching the skies for the two cranes you sent me.

Your waiting-for-the-cranes-from-Japan Maggie.

* * * *

PHYSICIST. Szilard and Wigner drove from Princeton to Long Island. It was a very hot July day. It was a very long drive.

WIGNER. He'll never sign this letter to Roosevelt.

SZILARD. He doesn't know anything about the work Fermi and I have been doing. Once he's read these reports on our experiments, he'll sign.

WIGNER. But you have no proof the Germans know as much as you do?

SZILARD. They can't be more than six months behind. In fact, if they're stockpiling uranium 235, then they're six months ahead.

WIGNER. Einstein hates war, Leo. He's not going to help make a super-weapon.

SZILARD *(stops the car)*. And I love war?

WIGNER. I didn't say that.

SZILARD. Hahn, Weiszäcker, Heisenberg.

WIGNER. I know who they've got.

SZILARD. They were our teachers. And you think they don't know what we know? They know. And soon they'll have all the usable uranium in the world. And then, that will be that. And Hitler will be dictator of all of Europe. Maybe even the whole world. *(Pause.)* OK, forget it. We tried. We failed.

WIGNER. Wait a minute, I think this is the right place. Peconic. I'm sure of it.

SZILARD. You said that three times already.

WIGNER. Four's the charm. I'm sure this is it. Now I remember.

SZILARD. Now he remembers. I'm going back. It's finished.

WIGNER. One more time.

SZILARD. No, I've had it. Just as well, nothing good ever comes from giving a government information like this. Maybe it's fate.

WIGNER. One more time, then we go.

SZILARD. I'm asking the first person I see. And then we go.

PHYSICIST. Szilard saw this young boy. He shouted:

SZILARD. "Hey, kid, you know where Einstein lives?"

ACTOR 3. "Sure, mister, he lives right down that street on the beach."

(WIGNER hands EINSTEIN the letter.)

ACTOR 4. H.G. Wells said in 1920, "Human history becomes more and more a race between education and catastrophe."

EINSTEIN *(reading a draft of the letter).* It can't be done.

SZILARD. We're not talking about tons of uranium; we're talking about pounds.

EINSTEIN. It still can't be done. The bomb would be too big. No airplane could transport it. You would have to float it on water and pull it with a ship.

(SZILARD hands EINSTEIN a drawing.)

EINSTEIN. Who did this?

SZILARD. Fermi.

EINSTEIN. It works?

SZILARD. It works.

EINSTEIN. Heisenberg knows this?

SZILARD. How could he not?

ACTOR 4. In 1914, H.G. Wells said: "Nothing could have been more obvious to the people of the early twentieth-century than the rapidity with which war was becoming impossible. And as certainly, they did not see it. They did not see it until the atomic bombs burst in their fumbling hands."

PHYSICIST. Szilard and Einstein argued the whole night through about the wording of the letter to President Roosevelt. Finally, after many revisions, Einstein signed it. The letter is dated: August 2, 1939, Peconic, Long Island.

* * * *

LETTER D

(The letters of the young WOMEN are interwoven, with one speaker not fully aware of the other.)

YUMI. Hiroshima, 14 March 1940.

Dear Maggie, I am worried. I have written two letters, and you have not answered. Are you all right? I know that war has come to you.

I think perhaps you are somewhere else with your school. Ev-ac-u-ated like the little children I read about in newspaper.

MAGGIE. Edinburgh, 31 May 1940.

Dear Yumi, I hope you got my last letter. It's been ages since I've heard from you. But overseas post takes ages to come—even Daddy's letters from France. He was saved at Dunkirk, thank goodness! Now he's been sent off again, to somewhere in the desert, North Africa, he thinks.

YUMI. I have sad news.

MAGGIE. Maybe when those cranes finally arrive they will be carrying letters from you in their beaks.

YUMI. Mrs. Hachiya's cats die. You remember I am sure how they always are close, like twins. They walk together on street and a car runs over them. Yoshiro sees it happen and tells Mrs. Hachiya.

I meet him at cinema next evening and he walks me home. He is very nice and I like him so much. One year older than me, 16, but I am one who feel older. He speaks of war in Europe.

YOSHIRO. "If they make war here, I go to be soldier,"

YUMI. he says. Boys can be—your favorite word—stupid. But only sometimes. Yoshiro teaches me how to draw. He shows me how to look at nature and see things for first time. Today we just happen to meet on Hijiyama Hill—remember we picnic there?—and he tell me how to look at cloud.

YOSHIRO. When you learn to truly see, you will see that light always comes from the darkest part of the cloud.

YUMI. So I choose cloud. I look at it. I find darkest part and imagine silkworms making it with threads of light. I pull all the threads of light apart and spin them back into cloud. *Now* I can draw cloud! When you return I show you how. Someday, we are both artists—

MAGGIE. Oh, Yumi, I wish I could hear your voice!

YUMI. famous artists, famous cloud artists!

MAGGIE. We have a new French teacher at school. She escaped after Dunkirk and came to Edinburgh. Her name is Mademoiselle Pinatelle, so we call her Peanut Shell—but never to her face. She is very sad and wears a coat and wellies even in class. I suppose she's not used to all our rain.

YUMI. Please, please write soon.

MAGGIE. And since coal is rationed now she must be freezing, coming from a lovely sunny climate.

YUMI. I worry about you and bombings.

MAGGIE. Mummy and I are just no good at stretching our rations. At the beginning of each month we make a good resolution, but nothing works. Worst of all, there's no fresh bread. They think we'll eat too much if it's fresh. Boring! and—of course—stupid!

YUMI. Next time, I draw big fluffy cloud and send it to you to make you cheery. Your worrying friend, Yumi.

MAGGIE. One of these days the postman, a girl who is a replacement for the duration and who actually looks happy to be doing the job, will dump a huge bag full of letters from you on the doorstep. Till then, I'll keep on writing to you. Love, Your dying-for-a-chocolate-bar— or—even—*two*-sweets Maggie.

* * * *

PHYSICIST. The next hurdle Szilard faced was how to get Roosevelt to read the letter. He contacted successful businessman, Alexander Sachs. Sachs was one of the few people in the world who had personal access to Roosevelt. Sachs took the letter to Roosevelt. He explained as best he could what the letter disclosed. Roosevelt listened, politely. He told Sachs...

ROOSEVELT. I'll think about it.

PHYSICIST. Sachs went home thinking he had failed miserably. He couldn't sleep. The next morning, very early, he went back to the White House unannounced. He took his chances about whether Roosevelt would see him again. They had breakfast together. This time Sachs said nothing about atomic fission and chain reactions.

SACHS. OK. It's like this: What if you're Napoleon and you're in the battle of your life, and this guy comes to you and says he's got a new piece of artillery that is twenty thousand times better than your current artillery, that his cannons are like machine guns against bows and arrows, the only thing is his cousin is making the same pitch to your enemy but the cousin's a few months behind in his planning? What are you going to say to him? Thank you, very much, I'll think about it?

PHYSICIST. Roosevelt summoned his personal aide.

ROOSEVELT. "Give this man whatever he wants."

PHYSICIST. The rest is history. It's called the Manhattan Project: the single most important, most complex, scientific-military-industrial achievement in the history of the world. General Leslie Groves of the Army was the overall director; Robert Oppenheimer, a physicist from Berkeley, was the scientific director; and the Dupont Company was the general contractor.

The Manhattan Project was an unprecedented undertaking. Neither Nazi Germany nor the Communist Soviet Union nor the Japanese Empire were ever able to achieve the extraordinary cooperation that characterized the everyday work involved in the Manhattan Project of these three great institutions of the modern state: the scientific community, the military, and the industrialists.

* * * *

"THIS IS YOUR MOMENT"

*(April 1955—Hollywood, California. A month before the broadcast of the TV show "*THIS IS YOUR MOMENT*" which will feature REVEREND MINAGA.*

The REVEREND and RICHARDS each stand on a chair downstage.)

RICHARDS. Can you hear me all right, Reverend Minaga?

REVEREND. There is a little static on the line.

RICHARDS. I can hear you fine. If we get disconnected, my assistant will call you back. *(Beat.)* So, what's your decision?

REVEREND. I'm still undecided.

RICHARDS. Why is that?

REVEREND. I have an important speech to give the next day at Berkeley. I have to prepare.

RICHARDS. You'll have plenty of time for speeches. Just picture it: 40 million people. It's a great opportunity!

REVEREND. Forty million people?! I can't even picture what 40 million people look like.

RICHARDS. My show is among the 10 most watched shows in the country.

REVEREND. And I've never been on television before.

RICHARDS. It's very exciting. It's your chance to tell the world, once and for all, your message of peace. It could be a healing moment—for both of our countries. Ten years after the world's first atomic bomb, the silence must be broken.

REVEREND. Mr. Richards—when you called me now, do you know what I was doing?

RICHARDS. What?

REVEREND. I was praying. Do you know what for?

RICHARDS. I'm sure you'll tell me.

REVEREND. I was praying that my trip to America could pave the way for peace. And then this question came to me that has haunted me all day: If it is possible to have a force in the universe like the atomic bomb that can destroy so much life and value in a single moment— isn't it possible, likely even...that there exists an opposite force in the universe that can *create* just as much life and value also in a single moment? And if so, what do you think that force might be? *(Small pause.)* And that's when you called.

RICHARDS. Must be a sign.

REVEREND. I will do your show, but under one condition: The focus must be completely on the maidens. I must be in the background.

RICHARDS. Why such modesty?

REVEREND. In Japan, my critics have said that I am on a mission of self-promotion. My credibility will be weakened if I am thrust into the spotlight.

RICHARDS. No problem. After all, this IS a benefit for the Hiroshima Maidens Project.

REVEREND. I also want to be able to ask for money for the project.

RICHARDS. Of course.

REVEREND. My Japanese colleagues warn me if I stay in America too long, I'll lose my Japanese ideas. That I'll trade in my Japanese soul for a shiny, new American one. But they forget, I went to school in the States. I have already lost some of my purity.

RICHARDS. I do look forward to meeting you and talking with you in person.

REVEREND. You know, Mr. Richards, if I can open just one heart to the possibility of peace, I will have achieved my goal in America.

RICHARDS. I hope you can open 40 million hearts, Reverend.

REVEREND. I'll start with one. Good day, Mr. Richards.

(They both hang up the phone. RICHARDS' staff person, BOB TYLER, gives RICHARDS a "thumbs-up" gesture.)

* * * *

ACTOR 2. Rising tensions between Japanese and Americans during the Japanese war in Asia culminated in Japan's surprise bombing of the landlocked naval base at Pearl Harbor, Hawaii, on a Sunday morning in 1941.

ACTOR 1. Shortly after 8 a.m. on December 7, hundreds of Japanese planes decimated 18 warships and 349 aircraft.

ACTOR 3. Over 3,500 men were killed or wounded.

ACTOR 4. America was finally drawn into "The Good War."

* * * *

LETTER E

YUMI. The tenth of September 1943.

Maggie, dear friend, How sad I am to read in long, long delayed letter news of your mother's death in London. How tragedy for you. She go to London to see friend injured in blitz. But good deed end in tragedy for your dear mother. I remember how she laugh when her pretty straw hat blow into sea day we picnic on Hijiyama Island. Oh, how I really wish I had the power to send Grandmother's cranes to bring you safe to Hiroshima to live with us. Parents send regret to you and your father.

I pray he come home safe to you.

I sign sad letter, Your ever true friend, Yumi.

* * * *

ACTOR 2. What use are bombs and anti-bombs,
        Sovereign powers, brutal lives, ugly deaths?
        Are men born to go down like this? —Jean Toomer, 1923

* * * *

LETTER F

MAGGIE. The first of December 1944.

Dear Yumi, Please take note of my new address. I'm
still in Edinburgh, but am staying with Cousin Betty.
Actually she's not a cousin, but we've always called her
that. Her daughter, Connie, has joined the Wrens and her
son, Martin, is a POW in Singapore, so we rattle around
in this big house. It could be haunted. But it's quite nice.
Not like our comfortable flat, but all right.

I still miss my mother very much and my father's letters
are still all about her. I was going to go with her to London, but it was the middle of the school term...
Anyway, Dad thinks if I had gone too... You know. In
every letter he asks, "How could you let her go alone?"

Stupid, bloody blitz. Stupid bloody school.

I had hoped to go to Varsity here, but now I hope I
never see another school as long as I live. Maggie.

* * * *

PHYSICIST. In the summer of 1943, when I was a grad
    student at Princeton getting ready to take my qualifying

exams, Richard Feynman, a fellow student and the most brilliant and eccentric person I had ever met, cornered me in the physics library john.

FEYNMAN. Hurry up. We're going on a trip.

PHYSICIST. I'm not going anywhere.

FEYNMAN. I already packed your bag.

PHYSICIST. You're so thoughtful.

FEYNMAN. And don't worry about money.

PHYSICIST. I'm not worried about money. I'm worried about my exams. I'm not like you. I need to study.

FEYNMAN. Forget exams. This trip is important.

PHYSICIST. No exams. No degree. No degree. No marriage. Rachel is already counting the weeks till we can set a date.

FEYNMAN. I guess I made a mistake. I thought you were a physicist.

PHYSICIST. What the hell is that supposed to mean?

FEYNMAN. It means you're supposed to zip the zipper on your pants. Wash your hands. And go with me without asking stupid questions.

PHYSICIST. Go where?

FEYNMAN. I can't tell you.

PHYSICIST. Why not?

FEYNMAN. Because it's possibly the most important scientific project in human history and when they said they wanted me to work on it with the best scientists in the whole world, I said I couldn't possibly do it without the knowledge and skill of my friend. Besides, Oppenheimer wants you.

PHYSICIST. Oppenheimer wants me?!

AGENT. OK, Feynman, time to go. Is he coming or not?

FEYNMAN *(to AGENT)*. He's coming. I said he'd come and he's coming. *(To PHYSICIST.)* He works for the government: top secret, hush hush, and all that baloney. I told him you'd come. I told him: I know a physicist when I meet one. I'm never wrong about that.

PHYSICIST *(to AUDIENCE)*. Feynman and I drove all the way to Los Alamos. My life was never the same again. I never got my degree. *(Pause.)* I never got married.

FEYNMAN. Degrees don't mean anything. Only knowledge, imagination, and passion matter. And anyone can get married. Look at me: I've done it many times. Nothing to it.

PHYSICIST. Oppenheimer appointed me to a study group composed mainly of mathematicians, theoretical physicists, explosive specialists, and meteorological experts. Our charge was to scientifically determine the ideal targets for demonstrating the destructive power of "the gadget," for security reasons, that's what we called the bomb, the "gadget." We determined that: 1) the bomb would produce its greatest damage by primary blast effect, shock waves up to one mile from ground zero, thus the ideal buildings would be those most susceptible to blast and fire; 2) again, ideally, these buildings should be densely packed together; 3) finally, the target should be of the highest military and strategic value.

Many of my colleagues opposed the very existence of this study group. They thought that we scientists should not use our knowledge in this way. I said to them: you think it's OK to build a bomb, but it's not OK to discuss the target? Some said they thought the bomb would never be built. Others said it would never be used. It was meant to be a deterrent in case we couldn't defeat Hitler by conventional means or in case the Germans were able to build a bomb of their own.

Our argument seemed moot, because the war in Europe was very close to being over. The Alsos brigade had captured Heisenberg and most of the other German physicists. Sam Goudsmit, our colleague, had reviewed, on the spot, the Weiszäcker papers and all the other reports: the Germans had no nuclear weapons, and they had no capacity to make any.

SAM GOUDSMIT (to an Army INTELLIGENCE OFFI-CER). "Isn't it wonderful? The Germans have no atom bomb. Now we don't have to use ours."

INTELLIGENCE OFFICER. "Of course you understand, Sam, that if we have such a weapon we are going to use it."

* * * *

LETTER G

YUMI & MAGGIE. The seventh of December 1944.

YUMI. Maggie, when will war end?

MAGGIE. The third year of this bloody war that separates us. I may not be able to write so often—and I do, even though so many of my letters never get to you. Does the Red Cross lose them? Do you even know I'm engaged? To Ian McAlistair. What else—a Scot. His ship is on the high seas, but soon he'll be on his way home, so he's safe so far, thank God. Betty's son, Martin, has died in the Japanese prison camp. Your letters are... How to say this... We agreed when Japan entered the war we'd never think of ourselves as enemies. That is still true. But I can't hurt Betty either. So I can't write you again... Oh, Yumi... If I write more, you won't be able to read this for all the tear splashes. Some day this terrible war will end... For now, please remember I'm still your friend. Maggie.

* * * *

ACTOR 5. In March 1945, American B-29s sought to bring Japan to its knees by pounding its great cities with incendiary bombs. The early bombing raids had a spirit of excitement and suspense said one journalist. The B-29s were lovely specks of silver against the summer sky.

(YUMI walks small toy kite up and down the stage, ultimately looking at the sky.)

ACTOR 1. Japanese citizens were ill-prepared for these incendiary raids. Civil defense fell on the women and elderly. Their fire-fighting equipment consisted often of hand-operated pumps, supplemented with wet brooms and mops. The great Tokyo raid in March 1945 began five months of bombing which killed more civilians than the five years of allied bombing in Germany.

ACTOR 4. By mid-summer 1945, the destruction of cities in Japan by B-29s was so thorough that General LeMay warned his superiors he would run out of targets by September. LeMay's bombers destroyed half the total area of 66 cites—burning 178 square miles to the ground. Lines of supply and communication were cut off.

ACTOR 1. The Japanese merchant marine was destroyed.

ACTOR 5. B-29 bombers ran "Operation Starvation"—an effort to isolate the home islands by mining harbors and coastal waters. Shipping, transportation, and manufacturing had ground to a halt. Japan was a nation on the brink of collapse.

* * * *

LETTER H

YUMI. The first of April 1945.

Dear Maggie, Finally, a letter comes. But it's really not a letter, just the envelope. Censor keeps letter. At least I know you write me. I have not much news. Yoshiro is long time in war, I do not know where. I only pray he is safe. We hope to marry when war is over. American planes bomb Tokyo, so I am very afraid for Hiroshima. People say, "Hiroshima not like Tokyo. Too beautiful to bomb." So many rumors. Day Yoshiro go to Army, we go to Hijiyama Hill. Yoshiro tell me,

YOSHIRO. "Draw cloud I take with me to remember you."
YUMI. So I draw beautiful cloud. Dear Maggie, I make much rain with my tears on little cloud. Sometimes I think we never meet again, Yoshiro and I, you and I. I think world ends before war ends. My parents ask we not write again till war is over. When people who live near see letter come from you, they ask, "Why Yumi writing to enemy? She not love Japan?" Of course I love Japan. But I never forget our days together. Yumi.

* * * *

PHYSICIST. We were all so focused on one thing: Stopping Hitler. We really believed that the Germans had a 50/50 chance of making the bomb before we did.

EINSTEIN. "If I had known the Germans would not succeed in constructing the atom bomb, I would never have lifted a finger."

SZILARD. "During 1943 and part of 1944, our greatest worry was the possibility that Germany would perfect an atomic bomb before the invasion of Europe... In 1945, when we ceased worrying about what the Germans might do to us, we began to worry about what the government of the United States might do to other countries."

PHYSICIST. Neils Bohr went to Roosevelt. Roosevelt listened politely, said he would set up a civilian review board to recommend policy on the development and use of nuclear power and weapons. But, he would make no promises about the use of the bomb. Bohr then went to Churchill. After listening to Bohr for one half hour, Churchill turned to an aide:

CHURCHILL. "What is he talking about? Politics or physics?"

PHYSICIST. Finally, Szilard went to Einstein. They each wrote to Roosevelt. Both documents were still lying on his desk, unopened, when suddenly, on April 12, 1945, President Roosevelt died.

(Entire ENSEMBLE stands in funeral tribute. They sing "Amazing Grace.")

ACTOR 6. In a speech scheduled to be delivered the day after he died, Franklin Delano Roosevelt had written:

ROOSEVELT. "More than an end to war, we want an end to the beginnings of all wars."

(The funeral tableaux ends. ACTOR 1 performs the ritual of sepukku to indicate the sacrificial death of the kamikaze pilots.)

ACTOR 5. On Okinawa, fierce fighting reigned from April 1 through the end of June 1945. Okinawa was a killing field. Twenty-five hundred people died every day. The Japanese lost 70,000 men. Eighty thousand native civilians perished.

ACTOR 4. Thirty-five thousand U.S. troops were wounded, and 12,500 lost their lives.

ACTOR 2. In support of the U.S. invasion of Okinawa, the Navy suffered its worst losses of the war. The mass suicides of the Japanese kamikaze pilots were a sight of wonder, fear, and great psychological effect. A news blackout of this daring tactic was enforced till Okinawa was won. For GIs and sailors, the kamikaze experience confirmed their fear that Japanese fanaticism would only increase as the invaders approached the Japanese homeland.

ACTOR 1. "Even if we are defeated, the noble spirit of the kamikaze will keep our homeland free from ruin. Without this spirit, ruin would certainly follow defeat." Vice Admiral Takijiro Ohnishi, sponsor of the kamikaze corps.

ALL *(chant-like)*. Kamikaze—Divine Wind.

ACTOR 3. Named after the typhoon which destroyed a 13th-century Mongol invasion fleet before it reached Japan—proponents of the kamikaze corps appealed to the pilots belief that death in battle would insure their afterlife as spirit-guardians of Japan. The pilots considered themselves the embodiment of the values of self-sacrifice and devotion to the emperor, and demonstrated that commitment with samurai-style hachimaki and swords during their final flights.

(In this section, science and history race against the clock. The facts come fast and furious, with increasing urgency and emotion.)

ACTOR 4. The U.S. began to plan for the largest amphibious force in history. We expected to encounter a totally armed and hostile civilian population ready to die for their emperor.

PHYSICIST. When Truman took the oath of office to become president, he knew nothing of the atomic bomb or of our historic effort to build it. On the 25th of April 1945, Secretary of War Stimson briefed Truman on the Manhattan Project.

On July 24th, 1945, at Potsdam, Truman told Stalin that the United States now had "a new weapon of unusual destructive force." Of course, Uncle Joe Stalin knew all about it, but President Truman didn't know that. In fact, Stalin knew more about our A-bomb than Truman did. Uncle Joe told Truman he hoped we would make "good use of it against the Japanese." General Dwight D. Eisenhower, our commander in chief, cautioned Secretary of War Stimson "not to use that awful thing."

ACTOR 4. The Enola Gay received its name only the night before the flight, named for the mother of the pilot, Paul

Tibbets. The crew of the Enola Gay had been specially trained and segregated from the other Army Air Force squadrons. The true nature of their mission was concealed until the last moment.

PHYSICIST. The hypothetical ideal targets which my study group had selected were now made very real. We were ordered to select four Japanese cities, using the following criteria:

ACTOR 4. 1) the bomb should be used as soon as possible; 2) it should be used on a dual target, military and civilian; 3) it should be used without warning; 4) it should be used on a "virgin," that is, on a city that had been heretofore relatively undamaged, so that the power of the bomb could be best demonstrated.

PHYSICIST. Ralph A. Bard, who represented the Navy on our committee, was the only person to register an official protest against these criteria.

I submitted my resignation to Oppie.

(OPPENHEIMER takes the paper. The ENSEMBLE loudly argues positions in support of the bomb.)

ACTOR 6. We had more casualties taking the islands of Iwo Jima and Okinawa than we had in the entire war in the Pacific up to now;

ACTOR 1. The Japanese are committing horrendous atrocities against our POWs;

ACTOR 4. They've killed millions of Asians just to impose their rule on them;

ACTOR 2. The kamikaze pilots, the ritual suicide of mothers and children on Okinawa, show how fanatic the Japanese are;

ACTOR 3. The Japanese don't make a distinction between soldier and citizen; everyone, regardless of age or sex, is willing to fight to the death, even in utterly hopeless situations;

ACTOR 1. The people of the United States are tired of war;

ACTOR 2. Our soldiers want to come home;

ACTOR 1. They don't have the luxury of debating ethics like you do in the safety of Los Alamos;

ACTOR 6. In the scales of Justice, a hundred thousand Japanese killed by an atomic bomb outweighs a million deaths, American and Japanese, in an invasion of the Japanese mainland;

ACTOR 2. The Soviet Union, and this is top secret, the Soviets are only a year or two away from making their own atomic weapons;

ACTOR 3. We need to show them our capabilities, our resolve;

ACTOR 2. Or they might turn on us in the post-war situation;

ACTOR 5. As a scientist in the Manhattan Project you have the same duty as a soldier in combat, to perform the job you're assigned: the scientific committee has been asked not *whether* the bomb should be used but *how technically* it should be used; do your job.

ACTOR 7. Our round-the-clock saturation bombing of Japanese cities, even our massive firebombing of Tokyo this past March, the single most destructive action in the history of warfare, hasn't moved the Japanese to surrender;

PHYSICIST. Oppie tore up my letter of resignation. I didn't stop him.

* * * *

LETTER I

MAGGIE. The sixth of August 1945.

> Dear Yumi, I had a disturbing dream about you last night. I have to write you, no matter what Betty thinks. *(Beat.)* Ian still isn't home. I'm sure his ship turned around and is headed for the Pacific. When I get too upset, I just stop everything and put the kettle on for a cup of tea. Do daughters always grow into their mothers? Maggie.

* * * *

ACTOR 6. Were there signs? Omens?

PHYSICIST. At the metallurgical lab at the University of Chicago, an organization was formed of nuclear scientists who opposed the use of the bomb. They formed a committee under the direction of James Franck to write a position paper, now called the Franck Report, which summarized the legal, moral, political, and scientific reasons why the bomb should not be used. This report was issued on June 11, 1945. Among other things, it accurately predicted the development of the nuclear arms race.

(The women begin a ritual of loss and mourning underscoring the PHYSICIST's text.)

ACTOR 6. There must have been.

ACTOR 3. Warnings,

ACTOR 2. things askew,

PHYSICIST. Even though everything was supposed to be absolutely top secret, we scientists knew everything. We had spent a lifetime developing channels of communication. We used them. I supplied the scientists at the University of Chicago with the information they needed to know about our target decisions.

ACTOR 3. the ordinary turned extraordinary,

ACTOR 2. foretellings of imminent disaster,

ACTOR 3. of doom.

PHYSICIST. We, the members of the scientific advisory committee chose the four targets: Hiroshima, Kokura, Nilgata, and Kyoto. When Dr. Reischauer, who worked for Secretary of War Stimson saw the list, he burst into tears. He went immediately to Stimson to have Kyoto removed from the list. Reischauer loved Japan, and thought Kyoto the cultural center of this great civilization. Stimson vetoed Kyoto. We added Nagasaki to the list.

ACTOR 6. A woman in kimono
      beneath a red and black umbrella
      whisked into air by a sudden wind.

ACTOR 4. The United States had virtual domination of the skies. Except for anti-aircraft fire, our B-29s seldom, if ever, encountered resistance by enemy aircraft at this point in the war.

ACTOR 3. A child running whose shadow faded in the grass and was gone.

PHYSICIST. The decision was made: The Army Air Force would drop "Little Boy" on Hiroshima.

ACTOR 2. A woman watering her window plants
      with water black as sin.

PHYSICIST. The Franck Committee, as it was now called, desperately tried to get Stimson to reconsider. It suggested a demonstration for representatives of the Japanese government: the bombing of an unpopulated island in a remote area of the Pacific.

ACTOR 6. A man who never dreams

ACTOR 3. waking,

ACTOR 2. screaming, from a dream

ACTOR 6. he can't remember.

PHYSICIST. The suggestion was turned down as presenting too many potential legal and logistical problems to be practicable at this point in the war.

ACTOR 6. Did someone pause on her accustomed rush to work
to look up at the dew-washed sky
and whisper to herself,
"This morning is too perfect,
too perfect in its sun,
too perfect in its clouds,
too perfect in its prelude
too perfect an ordinary day"?

PHYSICIST. The Franck Committee pleaded: at least warn the civilians. The Army lawyers responded that such an advance notice might be construed as an admission that atomic radiation might be similar to certain poisonous gases which had been banned by the League of Nations and which might make the United States government subject to suits before the World Court.

ACTOR 2. There must have been a moment

ACTOR 3. before the searing light,

ACTOR 6. the monstrous cloud,

ACTOR 3. the hideous black rain,

ACTOR 2. when someone noticed something,

ACTOR 6. a hint of hell to come.

PHYSICIST. I drafted another letter of resignation. This time, I tore it up.

(The ritual disintegrates; the letter is torn up. A new heroic beat begins.)

We christened the atomic bomb that was dropped on Hiroshima: "Little Boy."

Weight: 8900 lb
Diameter: 2 ft, 4 in
Length: 10 ft, 6 in
Yield: approximately 13,600 metric tons.

"Little Boy" used uranium 235 as the critical material. Inside the bomb, a modified smooth-bore naval gun fired a uranium bullet at target rings also made of uranium. At the moment of impact, a critical mass was formed, initiating a nuclear explosion.

I designed the gun and the uranium bullets. I estimated the explosive power of "Little Boy" in terms of the TNT equivalency of the blockbuster bombs we used in the saturation bombing of Dresden and in the firebombing of Tokyo. I did the best I could. I mean, a conventional bomb, no matter how powerful and an atomic bomb, no matter how small, are not comparable. With conventional bombs, radiation simply isn't a significant factor.

* * * *

"THIS IS YOUR MOMENT"

(A brash introduction by a TV theme interrupts the flow.)

TYLER. "THIS IS YOUR MOMENT," an American television phenomenon. Brought to you by extra rich Swell shampoo. The shampoo that makes your hair radiant when you rinse. And now, the host of our show, Matt Richards!

RICHARDS. Greetings, one and all. Tonight we are honored to have a very unique guest. As many faithful viewers know, we usually peek into the private lives of Hollywood stars.

But tonight's guest is a little different. His claim to fame? He has seen the future. No, he's not clairvoyant. He has no crystal ball. But he has seen the future up close—as few of us have—TILL NOW.

Our guest tonight THINKS he's appearing as part of a fundraiser for a humanitarian effort. What we HAVEN'T told him is—we are here tonight to honor HIS life, and the very important work he's doing. Let's bring him out now, shall we?

ALL. Bring him out!

RICHARDS. Good evening, sir. Please tell us your name.

(The REVEREND is stunned by the TV lights and response.)

REVEREND. Kiyoshi Minaga.

RICHARDS. What do you do for a living, Mr. Minaga?

REVEREND. I am a Methodist minister.

RICHARDS. And where do you live exactly?

REVEREND. Hiroshima, Japan.

RICHARDS. Reverend Minaga, please tell our viewers where you were...the morning of August 6, 1945.

(Pause. The REVEREND is confused and unsure.)

I'll tell you where he was. He was in Hiroshima, Japan. And what started out as an ordinary summer day... turned into a nuclear nightmare the likes of which the world has never seen. Reverend Minaga, are you familiar with our program "THIS IS YOUR MOMENT"?

REVEREND. No, I'm afraid I'm not. *(Sound of laughter from AUDIENCE.)*

RICHARDS *(laughing)*. I assure you, there's nothing to be afraid of.

Tonight we will reunite you with some of the people from your past. And we hope that you, ladies and gentlemen, will go away perhaps a little sadder and wiser, having learned what happens when man tries to play God.

But first, Vince Tyler, our announcer, has these special words for the girls in our audience. Vince?

(Lights dim on RICHARDS and REVEREND, as they talk privately off-camera. On another part of the stage, lights come up full on a shampoo commercial in progress, occurring simultaneously.)

TYLER. Picture a pond filled with glowing pearls.
WOMAN. Swell shampoo helps me find the radiance *hid-ing* in my hair!

> REVEREND.
> You said the focus would be on
> the Hiroshima Maidens Project!

> RICHARDS.
> It will be, and more.

> REVEREND.
> Is this a comedy show? They're
> laughing at me.

TYLER. Compare your shampoo with dreamy smooth Swell shampoo, if you dare.
WOMAN. There's no comparison. Just look at how my hair shimmers in the light. I can see the difference.

> RICHARDS.
> They're laughing WITH you. Not
> AT you. You're a very charming
> man, Reverend.

> REVEREND.
> But you're focusing on MY life!
> How does that help the Maidens?

WOMAN. Goodbye, dull hair! Hello, highlights!

RICHARDS.
We just want to give some background on you first. We'll get to
the maidens. Remember: 40 million people are watching. That's
a lot more people than you can
reach in all your speaking engage-
ments combined, isn't it?

REVEREND.
I suppose so.

TYLER. Swell shampoo. The shampoo that lets you...
WOMAN & TYLER. FIND THE RADIANCE, *HIDING* IN
YOUR HAIR!

*(Lights fade on shampoo commercial and come up full
on RICHARDS and REVEREND.)*

RICHARDS. Smile! Cameras are rolling. *(Beaming.)* Welcome back, ladies and gentleman... Let's take a walk
back in time almost 10 years ago. The day is August 6,
1945. The sun is just coming up in the land of the rising
sun. Reverend Minaga, what were you doing that morning?
REVEREND. The night before, I had noticed some weeds
in my front yard. I decided to spend the morning pulling
them. Later, I was to going see how my irises were doing.
RICHARDS. You never got to your irises, did you?
REVEREND. No.
RICHARDS. Why not?

REVEREND. I was—interrupted.

DANIELS' VOICE *(over PA system)*. The clouds looked like cotton candy. Out the window of our B-29, I could just make out the island of Japan. Hiroshima could not be far away.

RICHARDS. The sound of a voice unfamiliar to you, Reverend. But it belongs to a man whose actions have profoundly changed your life. You'll have the chance to meet him later. But now, your moment of truth has arrived. This is YOUR moment, Rev. Minaga. Please tell us what you saw on the morning of August 6, 1945.

(SONG: "GOOD DAYS")

REVEREND *(sings)*.

> I WAS HAVING A GOOD DAY, A GOOD DAY
> THOUGH I CAN'T REMEMBER WHY IT WAS SO
> GOOD
> I WAS WORKING IN THE YARD
> WHEN SUDDENLY—A FLASH OF LIGHT IN THE
> SKY
>
> AND WE ARE BATHED IN THE LIGHT OF THE
> BOMB
> WE ARE BAPTIZED BY SCIENCE
> IN THE NAME OF THE FATHER
> IN THE NAME OF THE APPLIANCE
>
> NEXT DOOR, A BOY'S FACE IS ERASED BY LIGHT
> DOWN THE STREET, A CANCER STARTS TO
> BLOOM
> THERE ISN'T ANY MERCY HERE
> THERE ISN'T ANY ROOM

ONE MINUTE I AM DREAMING OF A WOMAN
WHAT A FAITHFUL FRIEND SHE'S BEEN
AND THEN THE PATTERN OF FLOWERS ON HER
    KIMONO
IS BURNED INTO HER SKIN

ALL I SEE ARE PEOPLE SUFFERING
I REACH FOR A HAND—IT SLIPS OFF LIKE A
    GLOVE
THERE ISN'T ANY MERCY HERE
THERE ISN'T ANY LOVE

WE USED TO HAVE OUR GOOD DAYS,
    GOOD DAYS
EATING PEACHES BY THE SHORE
I ALWAYS THOUGHT THERE WOULD BE
    PEACHES
I ALWAYS THOUGHT THERE WOULD BE MORE

WE USED TO HAVE OUR GOOD DAYS,
(Spoken.)
    GOOD DAYS
(Sung.)
    AND TO THAT I SAY "AMEN"
WE MUST TURN THIS POISON INTO MEDICINE
WE WILL HAVE GOOD DAYS, GOOD DAYS AGAIN
(Pause.)

RICHARDS. When we come back, we'll meet some people who've helped shape your life. But now, here's a special message for you folks at home. Stay tuned.

* * * *

(The segments of the play start to blur as the sound of a plane drones under the sounds of the TV show.)

TRUMAN. "Sixteen hours ago, an American airplane dropped one bomb on Hiroshima... The force from which the sun draws its power has been loosed against those who brought war to the Far East. This is the greatest thing in history." —Harry S. Truman, August 6, 1945.

MUSICAL ENACTMENT OF THE ATOMIC BOMB

(The ENSEMBLE is thrown from their chairs, crawling to their next position slowly as the bomb noise recedes. Only the PHYSICIST and the PILOT remain seated or standing and unharmed.)

EYEWITNESS ACCOUNTS:

(The testimonies are intertwined, with neither witness aware of the other, but yet they are working together. The testimony is simple, understated.)

FR. JOHN. August 6th began in a bright, clear, summer morning. I had just finished saying mass.

SR. THERESIA. I wasn't feeling well, so I went to Mother Superior to tell her I couldn't take care of the children.

FR. JOHN. About 7:00 a.m. there was an air-raid alarm.

SR. THERESIA. We were used to them.

FR. JOHN. Almost daily, American reconnaissance planes flew over the city.

SR. THERESIA. Mother Superior said I should not go to the infirmary. She said I should go into the garden to breathe the fresh air and meditate.

FR. JOHN. From the window of my study, I have a wonderful view down the valley to the edge of the city. I could make out two or three airplanes on the horizon.

SR. THERESIA. In the garden I could hear the observation planes. Everyday the American planes passed over the city but none of them ever dropped a bomb.

FR. JOHN. Many people wondered why we were spared when the cities all around us were being destroyed.

SR. THERESIA. There were fantastic rumors that the Americans had something special in mind for us.

FR. JOHN. Sometimes the airplanes dropped leaflets which said: Surrender or Face Serious Consequences.

SR. THERESIA. The sirens wail the "all clear."

BOTH. Suddenly ...

FR. JOHN. ... the whole valley is filled by light.

SR. THERESIA. ... a strange, blinding light hurts my eyes. I don't know what this light is but I know it cannot be good. I run to find my children. A great blast of heat pushes me ...

FR. JOHN. ... a wave of heat pushes past me through the window. Then I hear the boom of an explosion which seems to come from a great distance, but at the same time the windows surrounding me break in a loud crash.

SR. THERESIA. The blast of heat must have knocked me unconscious because I found myself on the ground with my face in the garden dirt.

FR. JOHN. I am bleeding from cuts about the hands and head. I attempt to get out of the study but the door has been forced outward by the air pressure and has become jammed.

SR. THERESIA. I pick myself up. I don't feel anything. I am desperate to find my children.

FR. JOHN. I'm bleeding, but I don't feel anything.

SR. THERESIA. I run to the refectory. They're not there. Three of the support beams have fallen into the center of the room.

FR. JOHN. I force open the door. The bookshelves in the hallway have tumbled down. All the windows are broken. I work my way to the front porch of the novitiate.

SR. THERESIA. I find them. All my children. In the classroom.

FR. JOHN. From the porch, I can see down into the valley. Several peasant homes are on fire and the woods on the opposite side of the valley are aflame.

SR. THERESIA. I find them. All my children. In the classroom.

FR. JOHN. I run down the monastery road to help my neighbors put out the fires.

SR. THERESIA. I have found my children.

FR. JOHN. A strange storm comes up. It starts to rain.

SR. THERESIA. My children. Each one of them.

FR. JOHN. The raindrops are black.

SR. THERESIA. Every one of my children is a carbonized doll.

FR. JOHN. This black rain is very warm and unpleasant.

SR. THERESIA. I look at my hands. They are flesh. I touch my face. It is flesh. A storm comes up. The wind rushes through the classroom. Each child stands firm, a blackened statue against the ferocious wind. A black rain stains my flesh.

PERSONAL TESTIMONY

(The ENSEMBLE pulls themselves off the floor during the following.)

ACTOR 7. On the morning following the blast, I bandaged my head and returned to the worksite my students were working the previous day. Many eyeballs had popped out. Mouths were ripped open by the bomb, faces and hair gone, clothes burned over completely. It was just like a scene in hell.

ACTOR 6. Half-naked, bleeding, and burned survivors streamed from the city in a steady pace.

ACTOR 5. I have nothing to put in the grave: no body, no clothes. How can I bury him? What will be his body: in earth? in water? in sky? in fire? The fields need his nourishment. What terrible karma have we brought to life?

ACTOR 6. Relief parties moving into the devastated areas found few to rescue. The largest task was the disposal of tens of thousands of corpses. Some were buried in rubble—having died instantaneously. Those unlucky enough to have lived for a moment or an hour were piled deep on bridges, along the banks, or floating—where they had sought to escape the inferno.

ACTOR 3. I dressed Umito in his brother's nightshirt I found in the rubble of our home. I put his uniform trousers over the nightshirt. I found blankets to cover him and his brothers—the last gesture of love I could make for my children. We stacked wood on their bodies. I said a small prayer, and touched the match to the four corners of the pile.

* * * *

*(A sudden and profound change of mood to the imper-
sonal, "objective.")*

ACTOR 5. Robert Brode, American physicist at Los Alamos:

ACTOR 3. Willie Higginbotham, American scientist at Los
Alamos, in a letter to his mother:

ACTOR 5. "We were naturally shocked by the effect our
weapon had produced, and in particular because the
bomb had been dropped in the center of town.

ACTOR 3. "I am not a bit proud of the job we have
done...the only reason for doing it was to beat the rest
of the world to the draw...perhaps this is so devastating
that man will be forced to be peaceful.

ACTOR 5. "But if I am to tell the whole truth I must con-
fess that our relief was really greater than our horror...

ACTOR 3. "The alternative to peace is now unthinkable.

ACTOR 5. "Speaking for myself, I can say that I had no
feelings of guilt."

ACTOR 3. "But unfortunately there will always be some
who don't think... I am afraid that Ghandhi is the only
real disciple of Christ at present...anyway its over for
now and God give us strength in the future. Love, Will."

PHYSICIST. We were in a big study hall when we found out.
Someone shouted: "It's a boy." That was the security code
for a successful explosion. "It's a boy" to signal that the
bomb worked; "It's a girl" to signal it didn't. Since I had
worked on the timing device, accurate to one millionth of a
second, I jumped up and started going wild with my "war
whoops." I was ecstatic: maybe you don't understand. It's
one thing to successfully explode a stationary atomic bomb,
quite another a moving bomb, a bomb that you drop from
20,000 feet from a moving airplane. Champagne ap-

peared magically out of nowhere. One of the physicists had secretly wired the Sangre de Cristo Mountains with fireworks. He threw the switch. It was an incredible display.

Then, all of a sudden, I got very tired. Maybe it was the champagne. I was so glad the war was over. I felt such relief. I went out into the cold desert air, I walked toward the mountains, the Blood of Christ Mountains... for the first time the irony in this name struck this lapsed Catholic.

I started to cry. I never cry. It felt very weird. This great sadness had swelled up inside me: it overflowed into tears. I remembered Trinity: the searing light; the hot blast on my face; the mushroom cloud... I walked further out into the desert. I wondered about the people of Hiroshima. I didn't feel any guilt. I felt something totally beyond guilt. What happens to people when an atomic bomb explodes a hundred feet from their home, a thousand feet, a mile? What happens to people?

I prayed, I don't know to what or for what... but I prayed.

PHYSICIST *(takes book from sandbox)*. This is the full text of the Bhagavad-Gita that Oppie recalled when he first saw the searing light:

"If the radiance of a thousand suns were to burst into the skies, that would be the splendor of the Mighty One. I am become Death: Destroyer of Worlds." *(Closes book.)*

"I am become Death, Destroyer of Worlds."

END OF ACT ONE

ACT TWO

"I Am Become Light: Maker of Life"

(*The chairs remain in disarray as Act Two begins, very different from the orderly row of chairs at the top of the show.*)

PHYSICIST INTRODUCES GENERAL GROVES

PHYSICIST. General Leslie R. Groves, director of the Manhattan Project, before the U.S. Senate Special Committee on Atomic Energy, 29 November 1945.

General Groves, What happens to a typical casualty of radiation?

GROVES. "He can have enough so that he will be killed instantly. He can have a smaller amount which will cause him to die rather soon, as I understand from the doctors, without undue suffering. In fact, they say it is a very pleasant way to die."

(*Two ENSEMBLE MEMBERS play this scene over the overturned chairs.*)

PHYSICIST. This "very pleasant way to die" took the life of my friend and colleague Louis Slotin. Louie was a Canadian. His parents were Jews from Russia who emigrated to Canada to escape the pogroms. The Army wouldn't issue Louie a security clearance to work with me at Los Alamos because he was a "foreigner." Richard Feynman threw one of his classic anti-authority temper tantrums successfully compromising every security arrangement at Los Alamos, leaving notes to General Groves in every top-secret file advising him of the superb qualifications of Dr. Louis Slotin. Three days later, Louie and I were working side by side. Oppenheimer gave Louie the job of making sure all the internal components and mechanisms of the bomb would work properly together. I worked with Louie on the interior systems of "Little Boy" and "Fat Man," building the timing, measuring, and triggering devices.

Louie never wore any protective clothing. He used only two tools: two screwdrivers.

PHYSICIST. That's close enough.

SLOTIN. It's not even close to "crit."

PHYSICIST. It's close enough. The "Long Hairs" have worked out the math very well.

SLOTIN. Long Hairs know theory. This baby isn't a theory: It's got screws and rings and rods. The grease from my fingertips slows down the flow of neutrons. Did the "Long Hairs" account for that in their calculations?

PHYSICIST (alarmed). Now that's really too close!

SLOTIN. Isn't it beautiful? Makes me understand why a moth enters the flame. It's so beautiful.

PHYSICIST. A fraction of a second more and we would've been fried.

SLOTIN. One millisecond to be exact. One millisecond is exactly the difference between fission and fizzle. It's only by "twisting the dragon's tail" that I'm going to find out the precise tolerances. You know a better way?

PHYSICIST *(to AUDIENCE)*. In order to ensure a successful detonation, Louie had to experimentally determine the speed at which the two hemispheres of uranium would have to collide and the exact scattering angle and range of the neutrons. With his two screwdrivers, Louie slowly moved the two spheres towards each other along a suspended rod. He had constructed very sensitive instruments to record the radiation produced at each critical point. Louie had incredible concentration. His hands were rock-sure steady. The color of the radiated light told him when to disengage the two hemispheres to prevent irreversible chain reaction.

That's close enough, Louie!

SLOTIN. One more twist. *(One of the screwdrivers drops from SLOTIN's hand.)*

PHYSICIST *(shielding his eyes)*. LOUIE! *(To AUDIENCE.)* The whole room was awash in a brilliant blue-white light. Louie tore the two hemispheres apart with his bare hands.

SLOTIN. You'll be all right, but I'm a dead man. Got a cigarette?

PHYSICIST *(to AUDIENCE)*. By placing his hands between the two spheres, Louie stopped the reaction, thus saving my life and the lives of all the other people in the lab.

It took Louie nine days to die. It was an ugly, hideously painful death indelibly etched in my eyes, in my mind, in my heart.

General Leslie R. Groves testifying before the U.S. Senate Special Committee on Atomic Energy:

(ALL, at separate intervals, repeat GROVES' speech.)

GROVES. "He can have enough so that he will be killed instantly. He can have a smaller amount which will cause him to die rather soon, as I understand from the doctors, without undue suffering. In fact, they say it is a very pleasant way to die.

PHYSICIST. Louie's death brought me to Hiroshima. I needed to see for myself what the bomb I made had done.

* * * *

"THIS IS YOUR MOMENT"

(Actors move to stand on chairs as the TV studio is restored.)

RICHARDS *(speaking directly into "TV camera")*. Welcome back, ladies and gentlemen. In that hellish moment when the atomic bomb blossomed over Hiroshima like some godforsaken flower—100,000 lives drew to an abrupt close. Reverend Minaga, wasn't there some kind of warning to the people of Hiroshima that disaster was about to strike?

REVEREND. Not really. Unless you count the leaflets dropped from American planes over Hiroshima.

RICHARDS. What did the leaflets say?

REVEREND. They said: Surrender or extreme measures will be taken. They said nothing about the atomic bomb.

RICHARDS. Nothing?

REVEREND. Nothing.

RICHARDS. I can only imagine what it must be like for you, Reverend. To stand here, knowing how lives have been devastated. And yet you don't seem angry.

REVEREND. You know, in Japan, we have a special word; NIN GEN. It means "the person or thing that makes you human." Do you have an equivalent term here?

RICHARDS. No. I don't believe we do.

REVEREND. That's too bad. It's a beautiful concept, don't you think? In Japan, we don't believe a person is *born* human. We feel it is something you *become. (Beat.)* What makes you human, Mr. Edwards?

RICHARDS. Frankly, I prefer to keep the focus on you.

REVEREND. I'm sure you do. My point is that even trage-dies can be the source of great good. Everything in my life is a teacher to me. Anger, in and of itself, is not useful.

(SONG: "I'M NOT ANGRY, I'M JAPANESE")

REVEREND *(sings)*.
    DO I HATE AMERICA?
    I DO NOT HAVE THE TIME
    THE LIFE OF A FLOWER IS SHORT
    SO IS MINE

LIFE ISN'T EASY
WHEN YOU'VE BEEN TOUCHED BY LIGHT
WHEN YOU'RE MARRIED TO THE BOMB
WHO HAS THE TIME?
WHO HAS THE TIME?

(Brief interlude.)

I'M NOT ANGRY, I'M JAPANESE
IT'S NOT MY WAY
"SHIKATA GA-NAI"—IT CAN'T BE HELPED
WE WERE AT WAR

PERHAPS ONE DAY A COUNTRY WILL COME
    ALONG
EAGER TO ENTER THE FUTURE
EAGER TO DROP THE BOMB.
AND IF THAT BOMB SHOULD LAND
IN YOUR OWN BACK YARD
(Spoken.)
DON'T TAKE IT SO HARD
REMEMBER WHAT SOMEONE ONCE SAID TO ME:
(Sung.)
"DON'T TAKE IT PERSONALLY
(Spoken.)
TAKE IT IN THE SPIRIT IT WAS INTENDED
(Sung.)
TAKE IT LIKE AN AMERICAN
(Spoken.)
TAKE IT ANY WAY YOU CAN
(Sung.)
I'M NOT ANGRY
WELL MAYBE I AM"

(Brief pause.)

> **"THINK ABOUT THE LIVES THAT WERE SPARED**
> **DON'T THINK ABOUT THE COST**
> **THINK OF THE GREATER GOOD, NOT YOUR**
>   **NEIGHBORHOOD**
> **NOT WHAT YOU ... LOST."**

(Pause.)

RICHARDS. When we come back, Reverend Minaga, you'll
have the chance to meet someone who's had a great impact on your life. Stay tuned.

* * * *

(The PHYSICIST moves through the disarray of chairs.)

PHYSICIST. The city of Hiroshima is situated on the
broad, flat delta of the Ota River, which has seven chan-
nel outlets dividing the city into six islands. The city is
almost entirely flat and only slightly above sea level.
There is no marked separation of commercial, industrial,
and residential zones. Seventy-five percent of the population is concentrated in the densely built-up area in the
center of the city. When the bomb was dropped approximately 255,000 people were living and working in Hiroshima, most of them in the central area.

My first day in Hiroshima, I walked through the devastated city. I found a lunch box. Inside are the carbonized
remains of sweet green peas and polished rice. Months
later, I found out it had belonged to Reiko Watanabe, a

first-year student at the Municipal Girl's High School in Hiroshima about a half-mile from the center of the city. This lunch box is the only trace of Reiko that has ever been found.

* * * *

LETTER J

MAGGIE. The fifteenth of August 1945.

Dear, dear Yumi, For days I've been trying to write this letter. Ian has been reported "lost at sea." So the war's over, but what's the point, for me at least. Now the BBC reports that you have just heard your emperor speak. How must you feel? He was a god. You took me to one of his shrines, where people pray and leave offerings. How sad and angry and confused you must be... That hellish war. That hellish bomb. What has happened to you? to your parents? My dream about you. You're standing on your porch wearing plain white kimono. The sun is shining and you're laughing. Someone begins to paint a large black chrysanthemum on kimono. Suddenly, the sunshine becomes so intense you turn to run into the house. But kimono disappears and you are left with only the chrysanthemum imprinted on your skin... They do say dreams are the reverse of reality... Do you remember the once-upon-a-time-day-in-Hiroshima we cut our thumbs with a sharp stone and became blood sisters forever? Maggie.

YOSHIRO. Eighteen August 1945.

This letter to you on behalf your friend Tashahari Yumi. By very good fortune, she is not in Hiroshima when bomb falls. But parents die and house burn. She wish you happy life. Respectfully, Sergeant Takamura Yoshiro.

* * * *

PHYSICIST. When a person is completely vaporized by an atomic explosion, a shadow or silhouette of the person's evaporated physical presence is sometimes left on a surrounding wall or fence, because the radiation bleaches out the area not shielded by the person's body. The pattern on the person's clothes creates shadows of alternating light and dark gray in accordance with the reflecting and absorbing capacity of the fabric. If a person's body doesn't vaporize, the patterns of the clothes are burned into the person's flesh: a dark chrysanthemum, for example, would make a dark tattoo; a light chrysanthemum a light tattoo.

I observed the most interesting shadow effects up to 1.5 miles from ground zero.

From these shadow effects and other effects of the radiation, I determined ground zero, the hypocenter of the explosion. If you're anywhere near the hypocenter, the radiation simply tears apart every atom of your body. Ninety-three percent of the people within 1000 feet of ground zero died instantly, suddenly vaporized by a pure photon stream of radiant energy, by Pure Light. It's as if they never existed. Reiko's body was completely transformed by Pure Light. *(Pause.)* Isn't Pure Light our image of God?

* * * *

"THIS IS YOUR MOMENT"

(Again, the TV music jars the mood.)

RICHARDS. Like the proverbial phoenix rising from the ashes, Hiroshima is already rebuilding itself into a vital city, full of life and activity. But rebuilding the bodies and spirits of its surviving inhabitants will take more time.

MICHIKO'S VOICE. Reverend Minaga said that he wanted to help those of us injured by the bomb to receive plastic surgery in the United States. It was the beginning of "The Hiroshima Maidens Project."

RICHARDS. Ladies and gentlemen, we are happy to report that on Monday, May 8th, 25 young women from Hiroshima arrived in New York City via U.S. Army transport. The Hiroshima Maidens, as they are called, are being treated surgically at Mount Sinai Hospital at absolutely no expense to them. Tonight, it is our privilege to introduce two of these young women to you. Both have lived through the terror of an atomic bombing. Both have been severely burned.

To avoid causing them any embarrassment, we will not show you their faces. May I present Miss Michiko Minowa and Miss Keiko Emori.

MICHIKO *(in broken English)*. Hello, my name is Michiko Minowa. I am very happy to be here in your beautiful country.

KEIKO *(in broken English)*. Hello, my name is Keiko Emori. I want to thank everyone for helping us—to get our...operation. Hello, America. Nice to meet you!

RICHARDS. Welcome to our show, ladies, and welcome to America. Please share with our viewers how the bomb has affected your lives.

REVEREND *(in Japanese to LADIES)*. *Do datte bakuhatsu-o watashi tachi no jinsei o kaettemashita-ka!*

MICHIKO. My father managed a movie theater in Hiroshima. I spent many afternoons at the movies, dreaming that I would become an actress after the war was over. *(RICHARDS starts to interrupt.)* WELL, a week before the bomb was dropped, I went to a fortune teller with some girlfriends. The fortune teller told me: "You will be a girl who people will turn and look at." It was... how do you say...prophetic. Of course, I *thought* she meant I would become a movie star.

RICHARDS. That's a chilling story, Michiko. Have you ever talked to that fortune teller again?

MICHIKO. No. Many people in town were killed by the bomb. I assume she was one of them.

RICHARDS. When we talked before the show, Michiko, you had a very interesting comment about the light you saw that morning. Could you share that with the audience?

MICHIKO. I said...that the light was so bright...we knew it was something special.

RICHARDS. Something special. How ironic. What about you, Keiko? What has your experience been?

KEIKO. Like many survivors, I was disfigured by the blast. My mother encouraged me to wear a veil over my face when I went out in public ... so people wouldn't stare. But still they stared. Twice in my life ... my mother rescued me. The first time was on the morning of the bomb when a brick wall had fallen on top of me; the second time was when I walked into the sea. Both times, she dragged me back to life.

RICHARDS. Your mother must love you very much.

KEIKO. It has nothing to do with love, Mr. Richards. She is my mother; it is her job.

REVEREND. Each of the maidens has reacted to their misfortune differently. Michiko is a fighter. She wants to marry one day, to go out in public as she pleases, to live as normal a life as possible. Keiko, on the other hand, has had a more difficult time adjusting. She is among the *hibakusha*, the survivors of the bomb, who feel they are no longer entitled to human joy. It is as if they had become strangers to their own happiness.

KEIKO. Sometimes I dream that my brother did not die at Hiroshima. That he simply ... has been lost all these years, and that now he is coming home. So I prepare to celebrate his return. But he never arrives. Other nights I dream that a magical transformation gives me back my original looks. It happens just like before—in a bright flash of light from the sky. And when I pick up a hand mirror—I see my old face has returned to me! Then I wake up.

REVEREND. The Hiroshima Maidens Project is a humanitarian effort supported by both of our countries. American doctors and Japanese doctors working side by side to restore the Maidens to a more normal life.

RICHARDS. I want to assure all of you, there are Americans who feel it was very wrong to drop the atomic bomb on Japan. That it was an inhumane act.

REVEREND. We appreciate that.

(Japanese instrumental music segues in under dialogue.)

MICHIKO. Mr. Richards, there is something more we wish to say.

KEIKO. Yes, please.

RICHARDS. Absolutely. Ladies, this camera here will allow you to talk directly to the American people. The floor is yours.

(Over Japanese instrumental music, MICHIKO and KEIKO speak the following as if it were a poem.)

MICHIKO. *Once I wanted to be special ...*

KEIKO. *Exotic ...*

MICHIKO. *A beauty ...*

KEIKIO. *To stand on a ladder and reach for the stars*

MICHIKO. *Now we dream of being ordinary*

KEIKO. *Taking walks along the shore*

MICHIKO. *To fall in love and out again*
Fortune teller, can you see?
My hands no longer tell a story
I am the girl they turn and look at
I am searching for my place

KEIKO. *America, can you hear me?*
I am hoping for a cure

I am the girl who dreams of light that heals
Can you give me back my face?

Once I wanted to be different ...

MICHIKO. *Outstanding ...*
KEIKO. *Exceptional ...*
MICHIKO. *To fly in a plane to the rainbow's end*
    Now we dream of being ordinary
KEIKO. *To pass through a crowd unseen*
MICHIKO. *Maybe you can help us*
KEIKO. *Perhaps our hearts can sing*
MICHIKO. *Everything you do comes back*
KEIKO. *Make no mistake of that*
MICHIKO. *Each night we go to bed with one thing in our head*
KEIKO. *This ordinary dream.*

(Interlude of song, during which the following scene takes place backstage.)

TYLER. You're on in ten minutes, Captain Daniels. Are you ready?

DANIELS. No.

TYLER. Something wrong?

DANIELS. I don't think a person can be "ready" for a moment like this, do you? I mean, ten years ago, when I climbed into the cockpit of the Enola Gay—THAT I was ready for. Tonight—I don't feel so ready.

TYLER. But you're going on, right?

DANIELS. Sure.

TYLER. You gave me a scare there for a second. I checked your dressing room after the last break. You were nowhere in sight.

DANIELS. I went for a walk. I needed to think about some things.

TYLER. Promise me—you won't do any more thinking. We need you.

DANIELS. He's got to hate me, right? I'd hate me—if I were him.

TYLER. Reverend Minaga? I don't think reverends are allowed to hate. Matt Richards, on the other hand, is a different story.

DANIELS. What does that mean?

TYLER. He lost two brothers at Okinawa. But keep that to yourself. He doesn't like to talk about it. Relax. I'll be right back to get you.

(The HIROSHIMA MAIDENS exit the TV studio after finishing their song. They take off their veils in the corridor where they accidentally encounter DANIELS.)

DANIELS. My God.

(The MAIDENS quickly veil themselves; REVEREND MINAGA helps them to chairs.)

DANIELS. I'm sorry. I'm so sorry.

TYLER. Places!

DANIELS. I saw them.

TYLER. Who? *(DANIELS nods his head in the direction of the MAIDENS.)* Oh. You weren't supposed to.

DANIELS. Are there a hundred thousand more like that back in Japan?

TYLER. Captain Daniels! A lotta veterans are gonna be watching the show tonight. This is your chance...to clear the air, for all of 'em. Don't blow it. Everything's gonna be fine.

* * * *

(During the following presentation by the PHYSICIST, MICHIKO and KEIKO unveil in a solemn, dignified ritual/dance that reveals their radiation-distorted faces, arms, and legs.)

PHYSICIST. One of the most important differences between the explosion of an atomic bomb and that of an ordinary TNT bomb is of course the sheer magnitude of the energy released. An ordinary explosion is a chemical reaction in which energy is released by the rearrangement of the atoms of the explosive material. In an atomic explosion the very identity of the atoms, not simply their arrangement, is changed.

But, the greatest difference between a conventional explosive and a nuclear explosive, is the emission of radiation. The radiation is mostly in the form of: Light. The emission of light starts a few milliseconds after the initial burst of energy. The greatest number of radiation casualties is due to the ultraviolet rays, which have a wave-length slightly shorter than visible light and which cause "flash burn," a type of burn similar to the most severe sunburn. The flash burning, or carbonization of objects, particularly wooden objects, but sometimes of humans, occurred in Hiroshima up to a radius of 9500 feet from ground zero. The blackened sides of the objects allowed us to accurately determine the precise hypocenter of the detonation.

* * * *

LETTER K

MAGGIE. The nineteenth October 1945.

My dear Yumi, I was so sorry to hear of your parents' deaths. They and you are in my prayers. I'm sorry. I keep saying that and it's beginning to sound pat.

When I was eight, we lived in Australia, near a Carmelite convent in Melbourne. The thought of those nuns' constant prayers assailing heaven convinced me that God was a pushover for prayer. He is not. I have written your sad news to my father in London and I know he will be writing to you... We don't have much to say to each other nowadays. But why did Yoshiro write instead of you?

Please, please write. Maggie.

YUMI. The ninth of May 1946.

Dear Maggie...

(She indicates she is unable to finish letter.)

MAGGIE. The ninth of May 1946.

Dear Yumi, Please write ...

(YUMI dictates letter to YOSHIRO.)

YUMI. The tenth of July 1946.

Dear Maggie, I am only beginning to write—and paint—
again, so please keep patience. Thank you for expres-
sions of regret and prayers for my parents. I miss them
exceedingly much. Unlike what Yoshiro tells you, I am
badly burned by bomb. I go to live on island far from
Hiroshima to avoid angry people who say hurtful things.
But people flee cities after bomb, and many come here.
Nowhere to hide. Now I realize is wrong to hide. Next
war could end world. So I must work to let that not happen. I am yet too ill to join students who march for
peace. But know I must do something. First I remove
heavy veil I always wear. Then I sit in garden each day
and paint cranes on stone wall. People come to look at
cranes and talk about peace.

YUMI, MAGGIE *(reading letter)* & ACTOR 2 *(speaking).*
I say, "Look at me. I am what bomb can do to whole
world if another war come."

YUMI & MAGGIE. I make them look. Look at terrible
scars on face. On hands and legs and feet. Look at me so
they never forget. So they will march for peace.

YUMI. When wall is filled with cranes, I find another wall
and then another. It is my life now. Maggie. Yoshiro is
willing to marry, but I refuse. What is point if we can

never have children? The Yumi Yoshiro you knew is no longer.

Maggie. If only feel sorry for yourself, I cannot help. I hope you have happy life. Goodbye, Tashahari Yumi.

* * * *

(The ENSEMBLE hums "Amazing Grace" under the PHYSICIST's words.)

PHYSICIST. As I witnessed in the New Mexico desert, concomitant with the emission of light, a ball of fire takes shape and rapidly grows in size, expanding from the size of the bomb to a radius of several hundred feet at one second after the explosion. After this first second, the ball of fire expands and rises at the rate of about 30 yards per second, by mixing with the cooler air surrounding it. At the end of the first minute the ball has expanded to a radius of several hundred yards and rises to a height of about one mile. This rapid expansion of the fire ball creates a storm of fire with winds of 30-40 miles per hour. These great winds restrict the perimeter of the fire but greatly add to the power of the fire to do damage within the perimeter. In the center of the firestorm, temperatures reached 3,450° Fahrenheit. Wood and fabric burst into spontaneous flame. I saw the steel structures of bridges and buildings twisted out of shape. Objects of metal, glass and stone were shattered, melted, and fused. The Hiroshima firestorm destroyed five square miles of the city.

The enormous amount of material thrown into the air by the blast of the atomic explosion, the radioactive iso-

topes that had escaped fission, and other material irradi-
ated by neutrons, were carried high into the atmosphere
by the thermal currents generated by the growing
firestorm. All of this matter led to rain within 30-40
minutes of the bombing. The "black rain" as it came to
be known, carried the radioactive materials back to earth
in the form of fallout. The sticky, dark, dangerously radioactive water stained skin, clothing, and buildings.
Contact with the skin, ingestion through breathing, or the
consumption of contaminated food or water resulted in
radiation poisoning.

*("Amazing Grace" fades with the second "I once was
lost..." ALL ACTORS stare at PHYSICIST.)*

Official estimates of the number of mortalities caused by
the dropping of the atomic bomb on Hiroshima range
from 90,000 to 140,000. The official register naming the
people who survived the atomic bombing of Hiroshima
numbers 261,000. The Japanese call these people
hibakusha, the exposed ones.

The effects of radiation are not limited to those who
were subject to the explosion of the atomic bomb. The
physical effects of radiation linger in everything exposed
to the bombing: in the earth, in the air, in the water, in
people's bodies, for generations.

(PHYSICIST turns and sees ALL staring at him.)

* * * *

(The mood changes, with a quick look at history, science and the world to come.)

ACTOR 2. On 7 August '45, the Vatican City newspaper condemned the use of the atomic bomb on Hiroshima.

ACTOR 1. In June of 1946, Norman Cousins and Thomas K. Finletter, in an article in the *Saturday Review of Literature*, denied that we used the bomb to save American lives. They maintained that the U.S. government chose to use atomic weapons to prevent the Soviet Union from gaining control over Japan and to send a message to Stalin.

ACTOR 3. Also in 1946, John Hersey's *Hiroshima* gave a human face to the effects of the atomic bomb, making many Americans feel very uncomfortable with our continued involvement in the development of nuclear weapons.

PHYSICIST. In 1948, P.M.S. Blackett published his thesis that the atomic bombing of Hiroshima and Nagasaki was the first salvo of the Cold War, a carefully calculated threat to the Soviet Union.

ACTOR 1. Dr. Edward Teller proposes the development of the hydrogen bomb to ensure that the United States would be the undisputed master of nuclear weapons.

ACTOR 5. Robert J. Oppenheimer, father of the atomic bomb, opposes the development of the hydrogen bomb.

ACTOR 6. James Conant, president of Harvard University, issues this statement: "The extreme dangers inherent in the proposal wholly outweigh any military advantage... A super bomb might become a weapon of genocide."

ACTOR 4. Enrico Fermi and Isidor Rabi declare the hydrogen bomb to be "an evil thing,... wrong on fundamental ethical principles."

ACTOR 3. The General Advisory Committee of the Atomic Energy Commission unanimously recommends that we not proceed with the development of the H-bomb.

ACTOR 5. General Omar Bradley in 1948, said: "The world has achieved brilliance without a conscience. Ours is a world of nuclear giants and ethical infants."

ACTOR 2. In August of 1949, President Truman receives secret information that the Soviet Union has developed nuclear weapons and is testing them in Siberia.

PHYSICIST. In January of 1950, it is discovered that Klaus Fuchs, an anti-Nazi German physicist assigned to the Manhattan Project, has been supplying Soviet Intelligence with all the data of the Manhattan Project and with all the data of British nuclear research.

President Truman decides the Soviets are very close to the development of a new type of nuclear weapon many times more powerful and destructive than the atomic fission bombs. This new bomb is a fusion bomb which uses hydrogen as its fuel. It is dubbed the H-bomb or the Super Bomb.

TRUMAN. "I have directed the Atomic Energy Commission to continue its work on all forms of atomic weapons, including the 'hydrogen' or Super Bomb...on a basis consistent with...our program for peace and security."

PHYSICIST. The arms race, which the Franck Report had predicted, is on with a vengeance.

Nuclear and "Red Hysteria" sweeps the country.

In 1951, HUAC, the House Un-American Activities Committee, conducts "hearings" to purge communists from the arts establishment, from the entertainment industry, and from public education.

ACTOR 1. Senator Joseph McCarthy of Wisconsin joins the "witch hunt" and conducts "hearings" from April 22, 1954, through June 17, 1954, to ferret out communists and their dupes from government service, calling into question the loyalty of scientists, diplomats, cabinet members, and government advisors.

ACTOR 5. Robert Oppenheimer, father of the atomic bomb, science director of the Manhattan Project, and chairman of the general and scientific advisory boards of the Atomic Energy Commission, was brought before the Personnel Security Board of the Atomic Energy Commission on the formal charge of being a security risk.

PHYSICIST. Every physicist, except one, refused to testify before the security board. Dr. Edward Teller, the single exception, testified that Oppenheimer's "defects" of character and his opposition to the development of the hydrogen bomb made him unfit for security clearance.

In May of 1954, at the age of 50 and after more than a decade of distinguished service, J. Robert Oppenheimer was found to be a security risk and was removed from all his positions with the government of the United States.

ACTOR 5. In some sort of crude sense which no vulgarity, no humor, no overstatement can quite extinguish, the physicists have known sin; and this is a knowledge which they cannot lose. —Robert Oppenheimer, 1947.

* * * *

ACTOR 7. On May 11, 1955, American television viewers got a glimpse of atomic bomb survivors on the popular television show "This is Your Life." Audiences were both shocked and titillated as one survivor was brought face to face with the co-pilot of the Enola Gay, which dropped the bomb on his city. The next day, critics called the show "a new low in bad taste." Nonetheless, the show raised $50,000 for the Hiroshima Maidens Project.

* * * *

LETTER L

MAGGIE. Nineteenth of August 1961.

Dear Yumi, It's been many years since we last wrote. I can only hope you are still recovering and working for peace. I still have that last letter and read it when I get discouraged—which certainly isn't the case right now. What a summer this has been! The U.S.S. Nautilus tied up at Holy Loch here. What a reception! Young people—and some not-quite-so-young—came from all over Britain, all over Europe, to protest nuclear weapons. We sang, "Like the trees that grow by Holy Loch, we shall not be moved!" The police carried us away, and we returned to be carried away again. Your last letter jolted me into action. A slow jolt. I admit I was angry with you at first. Saying goodbye and signing your full name so formally. But finally I came to understand what you were saying: If we don't take responsibility, who will? I had to make a stab at making my own peace first. A quick visit to my father to try to recapture our old relationship. He lives surrounded by photographs and snapshots of

Mother. No room for me now... Being for peace and against nuclear weapons has not always been easy here. Why are people so hard to convert? Wouldn't you think ex-servicemen and women would have had enough of the alternative? But this last summer gives me hope. I really do believe we'll see a time when war is outmoded. I really do. Your peace-bringing cranes must cover a wall the size of the Great Wall of China by this time. Maybe you can take time off to write to me. Yours, Maggie.

* * * *

ALL. *Hibakusha.*

ACTOR 2. This is the Japanese name for anyone who lived through the atomic bombings. Literally, the word means:

ALL. *Exposed one.*

ACTOR 2. Currently, the government of Japan officially recognizes

ALL. 368,259

ACTOR 2. living *hibakusha*. Most of these survivors suffered acute radiation sickness in the days immediately following the bombings. In Hiroshima, the levels of gamma ray radiation in the air have been officially estimated at 10,300 rads and in Nagasaki at 25,100 rads. These radiation levels occurred up to three miles from ground zero. To put these numbers in perspective, serious radiation sickness begins at about 100 rads. Exposures at Chernobyl, for example, peaked at 500 rads.

For scientific reasons, in order not to distort the data obtained from their studies, it was the policy of both the Japanese government and the U.S. government not to treat the *hibakusha*.

ACTOR 1. A law was passed requiring all survivors to be registered with the government and to carry a special identity card declaring them to be *hibakusha*.

ACTOR 6. The law also required the *hibakusha* to report to the field clinics every six months for testing.

ACTOR 4. Not only were the *hibakusha* not treated for their various medical conditions, they were also shunned and ridiculed by their own people.

ACTOR 7. For these reasons, many people chose to hide the truth of their condition.

ACTOR 5. This situation continued until 1954, when 23 Japanese fishermen aboard the *Lucky Dragon* and 82 inhabitants of the Rongelap Atoll were exposed to fallout from the hydrogen bomb tests at Bikini Atoll. Spontaneously and uncharacteristically, the *hibakusha* took to the streets to protest the development of nuclear weapons. They also demanded that they be given proper treatment for their medical conditions and that they receive monetary compensation from the government of Japan for being casualties of Japan's war of aggression.

ACTOR 2. In 1955, the *hibakusha* organized themselves into a movement dedicated to peacemaking and to the banning of all nuclear weapons.

PHYSICIST. In 1965, William L. Laurence, the science editor emeritus of *The New York Times* interviewed some of the scientists who worked on the Manhattan Project.

Dr. Oppenheimer, knowing what you know now, would you do it again?

OPPENHEIMER. Yes.

PHYSICIST. Even after Hiroshima?

OPPENHEIMER. Yes.

PHYSICIST. Was it necessary to use the bomb on both Hiroshima and Nagasaki? Wasn't Hiroshima enough?

OPPENHEIMER. Secretary of War Henry L. Stimson and President Truman were sure that the choice was either invasion or the bomb. Maybe they were wrong, but I am not sure that Japan was ready to surrender. From what I know today, I do not believe that we could have known with any degree of certainty that the atomic bomb was necessary to end the war. Probably a settlement could have been reached by political means.

PHYSICIST. Dr. Edward Teller.

TELLER. To develop the bomb was right. To drop it was wrong. We could have used the bomb to end the war without bloodshed by exploding it high over Tokyo at night without prior warning. We could then have said to the Japanese leaders: "This was an atomic bomb. One of them can destroy a city. Surrender or be destroyed!" I believe they would've surrendered. But, I am quite willing to work on the development of the new type of nuclear weapons.

PHYSICIST. Dr. Eugene Wigner.

WIGNER. There was no difference in my attitude concerning the possible use of a nuclear weapon against Germany, on the one hand, and against Japan, on the other. In both cases my attitude would have been governed at that time by the view of whether peace could be obtained without the use of a nuclear weapon. I am now inclined to believe that the use of the nuclear bomb to terminate the war was a more humane way and led to less suffering and loss of life than any other way that was contemplated.

PHYSICIST. John J. McCloy.

McCLOY. I tried to tell Stimson to advise the Japanese that we had the bomb. I am absolutely convinced that had we said they could keep the emperor, together with the threat of the atomic bomb, they would have accepted and we would never have had to drop the bomb.

(The chairs are all returned to their starting positions. Order is restored.)

PHYSICIST. Why do soap bubbles cling to the sides of the bathtub? Why does a baseball always curve no matter how straight you throw it? Why do I ask why? What is it that I want to know? Sure I want to know how things work so I can get what I want, so I can protect myself and those I love from pain and suffering. But, it isn't just about control or power or convenience. I like to figure things out. I enjoy learning. I want to know everything I can, what all this is that we call reality or the world or the universe. That's all science is: it is a tool for gaining knowledge. It's a process, a way of finding out some things. Science isn't everything. It doesn't answer every question, but it does belong to the very best part of me, to the part of me that cares about knowing, the part of me that wants to know who I am and what it means to be human.

Yes, I'd do it again. I'd work on the making of the atomic bomb.

* * * *

(The ACTORS "break" the "fourth wall," and directly address the AUDIENCE.)

ACTOR 2. The Smithsonian Museum planned an exhibition on the Enola Gay, the modified B-29 bomber used to drop the atomic bomb on Hiroshima. The exhibit was scheduled to open in the spring of 1995. It was the intention of the Smithsonian staff to place this world-shaking event in its historical context. They knew this would not be an easy task:

HARWIT. "...the worrisome question is whether we will succeed in providing a historically accurate account of the atomic bombings and the end of the war. If we cannot mount a thoroughly documented exhibition, then we have little hope of learning from these epochal events. And if we are unable to draw wisdom from the war's conclusion, we will have marked its anniversary with a deplorable failure."

PHYSICIST. August '94. Martin Harwit, director of the National Air and Space Museum of the Smithsonian.

ACTOR 2. The Smithsonian staff completed a draft of the plan for the exhibition.

After reading this text, American Legion Commander William Detweiler wrote a letter to President Clinton accusing the officials of the Smithsonian of calling "into question the morality and motives of President Truman's decision to end World War II quickly and decisively by using the atomic bomb."

The highly negative reaction to the first draft of the exhibition script caught the Smithsonian staff by surprise.

In order to accommodate the concerns of their critics, the Smithsonian staff went over the 500-page script line by line with representatives from various organizations, including veterans groups and historians.

In these negotiations, the following items were challenged as being biased against the United States or offensive to American veterans.

ACTOR 5. all quotes by anyone who opposed or criticized the decision to use the atomic bombs;

ACTOR 1. all photos of dead Japanese victims of the atomic bombs;

ACTOR 6. all references to internment camps for citizens of the United States of Japanese descent;

ACTOR 3. all references to the arms race, to the problems associated with nuclear testing, to radiation experiments conducted by the Army and the U.S. government on U.S. citizens without their knowledge or consent;

ACTOR 2. any reference to President Truman's having qualms afterwards about the decision to use the bomb;

ACTOR 7. all references to the possibility that Japan was on the verge of collapse or seeking a way to surrender prior to the dropping of the atomic bombs;

ACTOR 1. all references to the firebombings of Japanese cities which constitute the single greatest acts of destruction in the history of warfare, including the destruction caused by the atomic bombs;

ACTOR 4. any reference to the possibility that President Truman might have used the bomb as a warning to Josef Stalin.

ACTOR 2. Even this revised script was judged by the American Legion and certain members of the U.S. Congress to be offensive and biased.

American Legion Commander William Detweiler commented: "The exhibit still says in essence that we were the aggressors and the Japanese were the victims."

PHYSICIST. Martin Harwit

HARWIT. "...fifty years may not be enough time to prepare the nation to confront such a history. How we resolve this fundamental issue will determine what we choose to remember about World War II... in our collective memory as a nation. George Santayana said, 'Those who cannot remember the past are condemned to repeat it.' It's a crisp, astute admonishment, but one that we may not fully comprehend. If we want to avoid the fate Santayana warned us about, we cannot afford to remember selectively."

ACTOR 2. The script was revised six times. None of the revisions pleased those who claimed to speak on behalf of the veterans. The exhibit was scrapped. The decision was to display the fuselage of the Enola Gay, its tail, an engine, and a facsimile of the atomic bomb it dropped on Hiroshima. The exhibit text addresses only technical details concerning the building, mission, and restoration of the Enola Gay.

On 2 May 1995, Martin Harwit resigned his position as director:

HARWIT. "Three months after the cancellation of that planned exhibition, the controversy still continues. I believe that nothing less than my stepping down will satisfy the museum's critics and allow the museum to move forward with important new projects."

"I don't care about having had to resign, but I really do anguish because the public will never see an exhibition which, in its own rights, was far more important than merely a museum director, a group of historians, or a set of veterans organizations. To have any claim to greatness a work like the exhibition we were planning to mount must adhere to fundamental truths that are beyond debating points and belong to all of us."

* * * *

"THIS IS YOUR MOMENT"

(The TV studio is restored for the final time.)

RICHARDS. Kiyoshi Minaga, resident of Hiroshima, Japan—that most Christian of Japanese cities—you yourself, are a Methodist minister. Today, you are an ambassador for peace wherever your travels take you.

Earlier on, you heard the sound of this man's voice.

DANIEL'S VOICE *(over P.A. system)*. Below us, the city of Hiroshima disappeared. I wrote in my logbook: "My God, what have we done?"

RICHARDS. You now have the chance put a face to that voice. He's here tonight to shake your hand in a gesture

of peace. Ladies and gentlemen, please give a warm welcome to Captain Timothy Daniels, U.S. Army Air Force,
who co-piloted the plane which dropped the first atomic
bomb on Hiroshima.

*(Applause. REVEREND and DANIELS are reluctant, but
do shake hands.)*

RICHARDS. Tonight, we've focused a great deal on the
Japanese side of August 6th. Captain Daniels, please tell
about YOUR experience of that day.

DANIELS *(a bit shakily)*. At zero two hundred hours that
morning, we had taken off from the island of Tinian,
flying a B-29. The three possible target cities included:
Hiroshima, Kokura, and Nagasaki. Shortly before reach-
ing the coastline of Japan, we got word: weather was
clear over Hiroshima. Therefore ... Hiroshima was our
target. *(Pause.)* At exactly 8:15 the bomb was dropped.
As we had rehearsed, we quickly turned to get out of the
way. Seconds later, we turned back to see what happened ... and in front of our eyes, the city of Hiroshima
vanished.

RICHARDS. Captain Daniels. You have since left the military life. Today you're a personnel manager at Sweet
Success Candymakers in New York City. You've had 10
years to think about that moment in the sky. What are
your thoughts today? Please ... tell Reverend Minaga. In-
deed, tell the world.

DANIELS. This is hard for me to explain. I mean, I'm not
a terrible person. I've had my share of nightmares.
But—

RICHARDS. Please, Captain. It's only a half-hour show.

(SONG: "TWO MEN WHO STEER")

DANIELS *(sings).*
> I'M NOT SORRY...I'M AMERICAN
> THAT'S NOT ALLOWED
> TO BE SORRY IS TO BE WEAK AND UNCERTAIN,
> TO BE SOMETHING LESS THAN PROUD
>
> DO I LOVE AMERICA?
> DO YOU REALLY HAVE TO ASK?
> I WAS THE PILOT OF THE PLANE THAT ENDED
>   WORLD WAR II
> THAT WAS MY TASK
>
> DO I HAVE REGRETS?
> NONE THAT I CAN NAME
> I WAS JUST THE PILOT, AFTER ALL
> I WAS ONLY STEERING THE PLANE

REVEREND.
> CAPTAIN, I WAS THE REVEREND OF A CHURCH
> IN HIROSHIMA, JAPAN, YOU KNOW
> WHILE YOU WERE BUSY STEERING ABOVE,
> I WAS BUSY PRAYING DOWN BELOW
>
> AS A REVEREND, I TOO, AM IN THE BUSINESS
>   OF STEERING
> I HELP LOST SOULS, I GUIDE THEM TO THE
>   LIGHT

DANIELS.
> ARE YOU SAYING THAT I'M LOST?
> I DON'T THINK YOU UNDERSTAND

REVEREND.
>   I'M SAYING THAT TOGETHER TWO PEOPLE
>   CAN SEARCH FOR A CLEARING...

DANIELS.
>   I'M HARDLY LOST, DEAR REVEREND...
>   HERE I AM

REVEREND.
>   YES, HERE WE ARE
>   TWO MEN WHO STEER
>   NOTHING TO LOSE,
>   EVERYTHING TO FEAR
>
>   I'M SORRY THAT OUR HEARTS WERE NOT
>   BIGGER
>   I'M SORRY THAT OUR COUNTRIES
>   WERE UNABLE TO HEAR
>   I TOO AM A PILOT...
>   I STEER

DANIELS.
>   REVEREND, I THOUGHT THAT YOU SHOULD
>   KNOW
>   AFTER THE BOMB WAS DROPPED AND A WAR
>   WAS WON
>   I LOOKED DOWN AND SAW A HOLE IN THE
>   WORLD
>   *(Spoken.)*
>   ...THERE WAS A HOLE IN THE WORLD
>   *(Sung.)*
>   I WAS ONLY PROTECTING MY COUNTRY...

REVEREND.
THERE'S NO NEED TO EXPLAIN

DANIELS.
...LIKE AN HONORABLE MAN

REVEREND.
TWO PEOPLE CAN SEARCH FOR A CLEARING

DANIELS.
**I THOUGHT I WASN'T SORRY...
WELL MAYBE I AM**

DANIELS & REVEREND.
**YES, HERE WE ARE
TWO MEN WHO STEER
NOTHING TO LOSE,
EVERYTHING TO FEAR**

**I'M SORRY THAT OUR HEARTS WERE NOT
    BIGGER
I'M SORRY THAT OUR COUNTRIES
WERE UNABLE TO HEAR
I TOO AM A PILOT...
I STEER**

REVEREND.
AND MAYBE WE WILL FIND OUR CLEARING

DANIELS.
AND MAYBE WE'RE NOT AS LOST AS WE SEEM

REVEREND.
HERE'S TO PEACE EVERLASTING

DANIELS *(spoken)*.
TO PEACE EVERLASTING.

DANIELS & REVEREND *(sing)*.
HERE'S TO DREAMS. *(Pause.)*

REVEREND. Captain Daniels, I would like to shake hands. *(Beat.)*
DANIELS *(startled)*. But, we already did.
REVEREND. No. We put our hands together in a meaning-
less way...to please our insistent host. We did not shake
hands. This—is shaking hands.

*(REVEREND extends his hand and establishes a mean-
ingful eye contact with DANIELS. DANIELS hesitates,
then extends his hand and clasps. REVEREND brings his
other hand on top, in a four-hand handshake. REVER-
END bows to DANIELS. DANIELS awkwardly bows
back. AUDIENCE applauds. Then DANIELS steps to the
side of the stage.)*

RICHARDS. Reverend Minaga, you have been tireless in
your efforts to bring these 25 girls to the States for
medical attention. I have no doubt that many of our
viewers tonight will want to share in your efforts for
world peace.

And you can do so right now by sending your dona-
tion—no amount is too small—to: MAIDENS, Box 301,
New York, New York. We want you to know that our

show's sponsor, Swell shampoo, would like to be first to contribute a check for $500 to this important humanitarian cause. Please, ladies and gentlemen at home, give whatever you can. This is YOUR moment. Good night. *(DANIELS and REVEREND freeze in tableaux of shaking hands.)*

* * * *

PHYSICIST. When Oppie was a student at Göttingen in Germany working on his doctorate in physics, he drove his colleagues nuts with one incessant question which he raised at every opportunity: "Why does Dante locate the eternal quest for self-knowledge in Hell and not in Paradise?" Finally, one evening Paul Dirac confronted Oppenheimer: "You cannot work in Science and in Poetry at the same time. You cannot do these two things together: Science and Poetry are exactly opposite!"

When I was a young man, when I first started working in science, I would've agreed with Paul Dirac. But now, now I know that Science and Poetry must be done together. That is the truly human way. We must always re-invent what we know, we must always re-invent ourselves, our worlds—every time we think, or will, or value, or love, or hate. We must because that's how we get to know and understand ourselves. If we don't understand poetry as the complement to science, if we don't understand science as the complement to poetry, then we are truly imprisoned in a world without a future, in a self without real possibilities.

When I was young, had I understood something of this truth, I would have known how to live my own life—as a scientist and as a husband, as a scientist and as a father, as a scientist and as a friend. I would've known how to live with two great passions instead of one!

* * * *

LETTER M

YUMI. The fifteenth of July 1995.

Maggie!

MAGGIE. Can you believe it, actually believe it!

YUMI. In one month you will be here! Standing here, at my door.

MAGGIE. I wish I'd thought to send you the occasional photograph through the years so you won't die of shock when you see a pleasingly plump—well, fat then—white-haired woman at your door.

YUMI. So many wrinkles now, they help to hide scars. But you will know me

MAGGIE. and you will know me.

(YOSHIRO helps YUMI to MAGGIE. Realizing that YUMI is blind, MAGGIE touches her thumb and then they clasp hands.)

ACTOR 4 *(singing "Amazing Grace")*. When we've been there ten thousand years,

ACTOR 2. Sister Theresia Yamada, Society of Helpers, survivor of the atomic bombing of Hiroshima, in June 1995— "I believe the use of the atomic bomb made the end of the war."

ACTOR 4 *(singing)*. Bright shining as the sun,

ACTOR 5. Ralph Triggiano, Aerial photographer, U.S. Navy in June 1995— "As I photographed the devastation caused by the atomic bomb, I could only think what a cowardly and unnecessary thing it was."

ACTOR 2 *(singing)*. We've no less days to sing God's praise...

ACTOR 4. In the *Associated Press* obituary of June 8, 1995 for Bob Caron, tailgunner of the Enola Gay, Caron is quoted as saying: "No remorse, no bad dreams. We accomplished our mission."

ACTOR 2 *(singing)*. then when we'd first begun!

ACTOR 7. Miyo Hayashi, a Japanese American, founder of the National Peace Academy Campaign in June 1995— "How could human beings drop that kind of bomb on human beings? '*Yuro senai*— I cannot forgive.' "

PHYSICIST. The full text of the Bhagavad-Gita that Oppie quoted the morning of the first atomic explosion reads like this: If the radiance of a thousand suns were to burst into the skies, that would be the splendor of the Mighty One. I am become Death: Destroyer of Worlds. I am become Light: Maker of Life.

When Einstein discovered $E = mc2$, he gave us a powerful light, a light brighter than the radiance of a thousand suns. With this light, we can see and understand the ways of the universe; what Einstein called the "mind of God."

Why are we afraid to step into the brilliance of this powerful light and look at ourselves fully revealed?

(The lights build to a crescendo, brilliantly illuminating the stage, the auditorium, and the audience, in this sequence.

The actors look up toward the source of the light.)

BLACKOUT—END OF THE PLAY

STUDY AIDS
Glossary

ATOMIC BOMB. A-bomb. Nuclear weapon that releases energy through fission, the process of splitting atomic nuclei.

EINSTEIN, Albert (1879-1955). Physicist. Wrote letter to President Roosevelt for government assistance on nuclear research.

ENOLA GAY. The modified B-29 bomber that was used to drop "Little Boy" on Hiroshima, Japan, 6 August 1945, 8:15 a.m.

FERMI, Enrico (1901-1954). Created the first man-made, self-sustaining nuclear chain reaction producing a controlled, measurable release of nuclear energy. This experiment took place on 2 December 1942, in a squash court beneath the stands of the football stadium at the University of Chicago.

FEYNMAN, Richard (1918-1988). Physicist. A stand-out eccentric genius among eccentric geniuses. Worked in the Manhattan Project.

GROVES, Leslie (1896-1970). U.S. Army general. Overall director of the Manhattan Project.

HAHN, Otto (1879-1968). German chemist, discovered nuclear fission (1939).

HIBAKUSHA. "Exposed Ones." Japanese term for those who survived exposure to the atomic bombs dropped on Hiroshima and Nagasaki.

HYDROGEN BOMB. H-bomb. Nuclear weapon in which atomic nuclei of hydrogen are joined together in an uncontrolled nuclear fusion reaction. The hydrogen bomb is a thousand times as powerful as an atomic bomb.

LITTLE BOY. Uranium fission bomb. The first atomic bomb to be exploded in an actual war.

LOS ALAMOS. National Scientific Laboratory. A research center in the Jemez Mountains in north central New Mexico dedicated to the applications of nuclear energy in general and to national defense in particular.

MANHATTAN PROJECT. Code name for the United States program to develop an atomic bomb.

MEITNER, Lise (1878-1968). Physicist. Developed theoretical basis for understanding nuclear fission which influenced the work of Otto Hahn and Fritz Strassmann at the Kaiser Wilhelm Institute in Berlin.

OPPENHEIMER, J. Robert (1904-1967). Physicist. Scientific director of the Manhattan Project.

ROOSEVELT, Franklin Delano (1882-1945). Thirty-second President of the United States (1933-1945).

STIMSON, Henry L. (1867-1950). Lawyer and statesman. Secretary of War, 1940-1945.

SZILARD, Leo (1898-1964). Physicist. With Enrico Fermi produced world's first nuclear chain reaction.

TELLER, Edward (b. 1908). Physicist. Key person for the development of nuclear weapons. Proponent of the H-bomb.

TIBBETS, Paul (b. 1915). Brigadier General, U.S. Army Air Force. Captained the Enola Gay which he named after his mother.

TRINITY. 16 July 1945, Alamogordo, New Mexico. The first testing of the "gadget," the code name given to the three atomic bombs produced by the Manhattan Project under the direction of J. Robert Oppenheimer.

TRUMAN, Harry S. (1884-1972). Thirty-third President of the United States. Made the decision to use the atomic bombs "Little Boy" and "Fat Man" on Hiroshima and Nagasaki.

WIGNER, Eugene Paul (1867-1950). Physicist. Worked on nuclear shell structure theory. Atoms for Peace activist.

Bibliography

BURNS, Grant. The Atomic Papers. Scarecrow Press, NY, 1964.

CLARK, Ronald W. Einstein: the Life and Times. World Publishing, NYC, 1971.

GILPIN, Robert. American Scientists and Nuclear Weapons Policy. Princeton University Press, Princeton, NJ, 1962.

GIOVANNITTI, Len, and Fred Freed. Decision to Drop the Bomb. Coward-McCann, NYC, 1965.

GROVES, Leslie R. Now It Can Be Told: the Story of the Manhattan Project. Harper, NYC, 1962.

HARWIT, Martin. An Exhibit Denied: Lobbying the History of Enola Gay. Copernicus, Springer-Verlag, NYC, 1996.

JUNCK, Robert. Brighter than a Thousand Suns. Harcourt Brace, NYC, 1958.

McPHEE, John. Curve of Binding Energy. Farrar, Straus and Giroux, NYC, 1974.

ROUZE, Michel. Robert Oppenheimer: the Man and his Theories. Eriksson, NYC, 1965.

SMYTH, Henry DeWolf. Atomic Energy for Military Purposes (Official U.S. report on the development of the atomic bomb: 1940-45). Princeton University Press, Princeton, NJ, 1946.

Internet Resources

Atomic Bomb Studies: General
gopher://earth.usa.net:70/00/News%20and%20Information/
mesharpe/military

Hiroshima
http://www.rerf.or.jp/Outside/ENG/Hiroshima/Contents.html

Hiroshima Survivors Directory
ftp://ftp.cdrom.com/pub/obi/Hiroshima.Survivors

National Air and Space Museum Research
http://ceps.nasm.edu:2000/PA/Departments.html

DIRECTOR'S NOTES